Resilience Begins with Beliefs

Resilience Begins with Beliefs

BUILDING ON STUDENT STRENGTHS FOR SUCCESS IN SCHOOL

Sara Truebridge

FOREWORD BY
Bonnie Benard

Teachers College
Columbia University
New York and London

Published by Teachers College Press, 1234 Amsterdam Avenue, New York, NY 10027

Appendix C was adapted from Vicki Phillips, *Empowering Discipline: An Approach That Works with At-Risk Students* (3rd ed.), © 2011. Reprinted by permission of Personal Development Publishing, US.

Appendix D was adapted from Jawanza Kunjufu, *Black Students—Middle Class Teachers*, © 2002. Reprinted by permission of African American Images, Chicago.

The author would also like to express gratitude for adapting throughout the book from Bonnie Benard and Sara Truebridge, "A Shift in Thinking: Influencing Social Workers' Beliefs About Individual and Family Resilience in an Effort to Enhance Well-Being and Success for All," in Dennis Saleebey (Ed.), *The Strengths Perspective in Social Work Practice* (6th ed., pp. 203–219), © 2012. Reprinted by permission of Pearson Education, Inc., Upper Saddle River, NJ.

Library of Congress Cataloging-in-Publication Data can be obtained at www.loc.gov

ISBN 978-0-8077-5483-2 (paperback)
ISBN 978- 978-0-8077-5484-9 (hardcover)
eISBN 978-0-8077-7297-3 (eBook)

Printed on acid-free paper
Manufactured in the United States of America

21 20 19 18 17 16 15 14   8 7 6 5 4 3 2 1

*Dedicated to all students of every age everywhere
who continue to expand my learning and capture
my heart and soul—all of whom will never be too
old to receive unconditional love and hugs—and to
educators at every level everywhere who have my
unwavering respect and admiration for possessing
the golden gift of having "the power of one" to
make a difference in the lives of others.*

I've come to a frightening conclusion that I am the decisive element in the classroom. It's my personal approach that creates the climate. It's my daily mood that makes the weather. As a teacher, I possess a tremendous power to make a child's life miserable or joyous. I can be a tool of torture or an instrument of inspiration. I can humiliate or humor, hurt or heal. In all situations, it is my response that decides whether a crisis will be escalated or de-escalated, and a child humanized or de-humanized.

—Haim Ginott, *Teacher and Child*

The path of least resistance and least trouble is a mental rut already made. It requires troublesome work to undertake the alternation of old beliefs.

—John Dewey

The world we have created is a product of our thinking; it cannot be changed without changing our thinking. If we want to change the world, we have to change our thinking.

—Albert Einstein

Contents

Foreword

Over a decade ago, when Sara Truebridge first walked into my office, I knew she was a force to be reckoned with.

Resilience is a compelling concept. The work I had been doing for over two decades began to have a following. This created a mixed blessing in my life because as much as I wanted to meet with every new convert, I didn't have the luxury or time to meet with every person who had come to resilience, whether finding my work through their own research, graduate education, or the trainings that I and others conducted over the years. Even though time was a constraint for me, she was not going to let it be a constraint for her. Sara was persistent in tracking me down. In an effort to appease her, I finally met with her. I was immediately struck and impressed by the energy, enthusiasm, and passion that emanated from her (not to mention that she had spent her adult life advocating for children and that she was just plain fun to be around). What I didn't know until she walked in the door is that I had finally found the person who I wanted to carry forward the torch of resilience.

Over 25 years ago I was one of the early pioneers in promoting the concept of resilience. The question that guided my work was "What can we as parents, educators, community members, and policymakers do to promote the healthy development and successful learning of our young people?" In 1986 I wrote my first synthesis of resilience research for the prevention and education fields on this strengths-based approach to working with young people. What this synthesis brought to light were the findings from several international longitudinal studies that had followed young children from various high-risk environments into their adulthood. An amazing finding was that children growing up in families of abuse, alcoholism, mental illness, and domestic violence, as well as those growing up in poverty-stricken and war-torn communities, can, and do, grow up to lead successful and meaningful lives.

As I continued to look into this research, it became clear that a consensus was coalescing on three critical developmental supports and opportunities that seemed to serve as buffers to adversities in children's lives and allow their healthy development and successful learning to unfold. In 1991, I wrote *Fostering Resiliency in Kids* that highlighted some of the research and identified this triad of protective factors found in family, school, and community environments. These three "protective factors" consisted of caring and supportive relationships, high-expectation messages, and opportunities for meaningful participation and contribution.

I naïvely thought that when people saw these research findings, policy would follow. I figured that policymakers in education and human services would immediately heed the call of research and focus attention on building these three protective factors in their respective arenas. But lo and behold— as is usually the case when bridging the gap between research and practice— falls the shadow of politics. As was then and as is now, we still have not created the policies that make children and those who serve them a priority. We still do not have a strengths-based, human development, and health promotion perspective. Rather we are stuck in a deficit-based, problem-focused, and punitive perspective. This means that we are still trying to "fix" broken schools, broken teachers, and broken students. If resilience research has taught us anything at all it is that schools, teachers, and students are not in need of fixing, but rather each have unique strengths and resources that need to be tapped, developed, and nourished. The most consistent finding in all of resilience research has been that a school environment rich in the protective factors of caring relationships, high expectations, and opportunities to participate and contribute have the power to transform the academic and life success of the students they serve.

As I continued to look at the research, it came as no surprise that the protective factors that research identified mapped very well to those factors identified in the research on healthy families, effective schools, competent communities, and successful businesses and organizations. Furthermore, when we look within ourselves at our own stories of how we got to be where we are today in the midst of our own challenges, we can readily see that good research is only validating our own experience and what we know in our hearts and souls to be true. This led to my development of a resilience theory that posits that healthy development in any human system depends upon a process that promotes the three protective factors, not a program or special curriculum.

In *Resiliency: What We Have Learned* (2004), I describe much of the research supporting the above ideas. I end my book with the conclusion that in any human system, including education, the resilience process starts with the beliefs we hold about the people we serve. I am excited that Sara's book starts where mine left off: Resilience begins with beliefs.

Resilience Begins with Beliefs: Building on Student Strengths for Success in School focuses in depth on exactly how we can create these transformative beliefs in classrooms and schools. Sara clearly delineates a process for doing preservice and professional development that can be sustained for the long term. Her book is based on her deep and unwavering beliefs that teachers are professionals and scholars, as well as the catalyst and key to the resilience process. She also strongly believes that many teachers intuitively know in their heads, hearts, and souls what it takes to tap a student's resilience and are already creating classroom environments rich in the three protective factors. For those teachers this book provides a source of validation for the good work that they are already doing and a resource to sustain their own resilience.

In this book, Sara provides clear tools, techniques, and strategies that can actually take a concept as elusive as beliefs and make it something understandable, concrete, and embraceable. Furthermore, this book is not only written for teachers but also for educators, administrators, and policymakers in education at all levels—federal, state, and local. In fact, I feel that this book would be a beneficial resource for anyone working within any human service system.

As I pass the torch on to Sara, my dear friend and colleague, I ask you, Dear Reader, to open your head, heart, and soul to the light that resilience theory and practice can bring to you as a person and professional in service to our most precious resource: our children.

Bonnie Benard

Preface

Resilience (re•sil•ience; ri'zilj ns; noun)

1. The ability to recover quickly from illness, change, or misfortune; buoyancy.
2. The property of a material that enables it to resume its original shape or position after being bent, stretched, or compressed; elasticity.

—The American Heritage Dictionary of the English Language

You would have to look long and hard to find someone who would argue with the statement that our children need to be resilient. In fact, resilience has become the word "du jour." Regardless of socioeconomic status, culture, race, or ethnicity, our children today face a host of adversities and stressors that they will have to navigate and weather as they grow up.

In the news or in the grocery stores, a day rarely goes by where we do not hear about some kind of adversity someone somewhere has had to face—whether it be because of a natural disaster, a disease, something done to someone else, or something someone has inflicted upon him- or herself. Stressors, adversity, and trauma are not relegated to certain zip codes. Adversity and risk such as physical and mental abuse, substance and drug abuse, domestic violence, crime, and natural disasters occur in our cities *and* in our suburbs.

When I was younger and teaching in an affluent suburban school, I was sometimes made to feel guilty for working there instead of working in an economically challenged urban school where my efforts would perhaps be more needed and appreciated. That guilt no longer exists. Today when someone begins to challenge me on how affluent communities have it easy and the kids from "those communities" have a sense of entitlement, don't need additional resources, and don't know stress, I bluntly share that I have buried kids from both communities—urban and suburban—and the tears I shed are no different. If you want a difference, here it is: The kids in the cities are killing each other; the kids in the suburbs are killing themselves. Whether it be from street fights or suicide, I have buried too many children. Numbers are meaningless. Burying one child is one too many.

It is naïve for us to continue to believe that a zip code protects one from adversity. Yes, we can have a discourse about equity and we can talk about the allocation of education resources in urban areas versus resources in suburban areas. But that is not the focus of this book. The focus of this book is to address how those of us working within our education system can tap and nurture the capacity for resilience that resides within all of our students—regardless of the degree to which they have been subjected to trauma, adversity, and risk—so that they are successful in their education and life endeavors.

With the support of parents, administrators, and policymakers, the goal of practitioners in education is to create, provide, support, and sustain environments that nurture the healthy development of whole students with outcomes that promote successful, healthy, ethical, and compassionate individuals who demonstrate positive growth and success in school and life. Fostering the development of the whole student means focusing on all aspects of students—their cognitive, social, emotional, physical, and spiritual development. This includes creating and sustaining environments where a student's capacity for resilience is tapped and nurtured.

Let me, from the start, make the following point clear: Understanding and focusing on resilience does not mean donning rose-colored glasses and denying adversities and risks. Adversities, challenges, and risks are part of life. Focusing on resilience means that rather than holding a deficit perspective where our lens is focused on risk factors—how adversity or risk leads to unhealthy development and unsuccessful educational and life outcomes—we take a resilience, strengths-based perspective and turn our lens to focus on protective factors: the personal strengths of individuals, the developmental supports and opportunities, and the environmental conditions and characteristics of families, schools, communities, and peer groups that mitigate and buffer adversity and promote healthy development and successful learning. It is acknowledging that with life come challenges and setbacks—sometimes small and sometimes big. Yet through them all, a resilience lens means identifying ourselves as survivors, not victims.

There are students who come from abusive homes, and some teachers who hold a deficit lens and only look at risk factors might say that these students are victims and conclude that they will have a difficult time meeting with success in school—let alone life—as they progress in their education. On the other hand, teachers with a resilience lens will approach the same abused students as survivors—they make it to school almost every day without us knowing exactly what transpired the night before or that morning. As compassionate teachers we will ensure the safety of these students and provide them with the same three major protective factors (also referred to as developmental supports and opportunities) known to mitigate and buffer adversity that we provide to all students. These protective factors include providing caring relationships, maintaining high expectations, and creating opportunities to contribute and participate—protective factors that they may not get from their abusive home environment. As we are able to reframe and recognize these students as survivors rather than victims, they too will identify themselves as survivors who not only received support from their teachers but also were able to harness their own strengths to "make it" through some very difficult times. With an understanding of resilience, we can shift viewing the world, communities, individuals, and our students through a traditional problem-based, deficit, pathology model to a positive, protective, and preventive model.

Education is not just about academics: reading, writing, and math. It is also about problem solving, perseverance, empathy, flexibility, creativity, confidence, decisionmaking, self-awareness, relationships, collaboration, and navigating to mine resources—many social and emotional skills and tools that are components of resilience that increase academic success. Research and information such as that produced and disseminated by Daniel Goleman (1995) and the Collaborative for Academic, Social, and Emotional Learning (casel.org) continue to tell us that academics and social and emotional learning are not mutually exclusive and that all students, regardless of being exposed to a high-risk environment or not, will need a combination of academic, social, and emotional skills to navigate through this ever-changing world. Yet today's education system is still having difficulty understanding and incorporating this concept. In fact, our educational system, with its myopic, short-term focus on tests, may be more of a contributor to stress than a buffer. This is another reason why the resilience of our students is so critical—it provides students with the capacity to navigate not only through the forces outside of the school that contribute to stress and adversity but also through the forces that contribute to stress and adversity that are found all too frequently inside our schools.

EDUCATION: A CONTRIBUTOR OR BUFFER TO STRESS?

Our current pressure-cooker culture, with our emphasis on "being the best," whether it be as an individual or as a nation, has permeated into our education system, creating a nation of public and private schools that seems to put more emphasis on raising numbers rather than raising independent, creative, responsible, contributing, ethical, and compassionate individuals.

As a student, teacher, legislative analyst, researcher, and most recently as the education consultant to the film *Race to Nowhere* (Abeles, 2009), a documentary that examines the pressures faced by young people, teachers, and parents in our high-stakes public and private education system, I have seen firsthand how our education system has become a microcosm of our pressure-cooker culture and how that has negatively affected students. Regardless of socioeconomic status, culture, race, ethnicity, or where a student resides, our students are pressured to produce and perform to a point that is compromising not only their learning, but also their physical and emotional health. Science informs us that there is "good stress" and "toxic stress" (Center on the Developing Child, n.d.; Mayo Clinic, 2010; Shonkoff & Garner et al., 2012). Our bodies respond to stressors with a stress response that activates the nervous system and specific hormones. This response is sometimes referred to as the "fight or flight" response. Two people may be exposed to the same stressors yet respond to them in different ways. One may experience the stressor as good stress while another person may experience it as toxic stress. I have seen this happen in the classroom. Good stress is what can encourage, motivate, and inspire a student to achieve a goal such as performing in a school play, doing an oral presentation in front of a class, or doing well on a test or exam. Toxic stress, on the other hand, comes from situations that are too intense, prolonged, or dealt with without the support of others. Being bullied, having a crammed schedule without downtime, or feeling like one test or exam will dictate one's future can have debilitating affects both mentally and physically. *End the Race* (Westheimer, Abeles, & Truebridge, 2011), the facilitation guide to the film *Race to Nowhere*, shares a reality all too familiar to many students, and that is that the toxic stress found in the corridors and classrooms of our schools has created "a silent epidemic that is running rampant in our schools. Cheating has become commonplace, students have become disengaged, stress-related illness, depression and burnout abound, and young people arrive at college and the workplace unprepared and uninspired" (p. 8).

Even dismissing the discussion about how high-stakes testing and the pressure-cooker culture have infiltrated into the schools, students are faced with educational experiences every day where it will be necessary to tap into their resilience. There will be a time when learning will be difficult and one's perseverance will be tapped. There will be a time when a student who had traditionally earned As gets a B or less and that student's optimism will be tapped. There will be a time when a student may have an interaction with a teacher or another student that is uncomfortable and his or her self-awareness and self-control will have to be tapped. There may be a time when a student needs to advocate for him- or herself to get some support in a subject area or with some services that the school has to offer and his or her confidence and communication skills will be tapped. Perseverance, coping, self-awareness, self-control, confidence, and communication are just a few of the personal strengths that both support one's resilience and are products of one's resilience.

It's time we really listen to our students. Our students' stories provide us with their voices that all too often are dismissed and not included in discussions on how to make our schools a place where all individuals are embraced and an authentic love of learning is fostered rather than thwarted. Kristen Olson's book *Wounded by School* (Olson, 2009) is a must-read for anyone who may question the adverse effect that many of today's schools have on our students.

WHAT CAN WE DO?

We know more than ever before about positive child, youth, and human development and how to best serve our young people. We also have research and literature that provide us with increased awareness and empirical evidence of the effectiveness of approaches available to optimize the resilience and hence the education and life experiences and outcomes of students. These "approaches" do not cost extra money but rather focus on re-culturing schools in a unified vision creating, nurturing, and sustaining important protective factors—the internal and external developmental supports and opportunities that all children and youth need—which provide a positive influence and buffer students from adversity, threat, stress, and risk. These are the same protective factors that create supportive environments that nurture, support, and sustain students' resilience and promote their health, well-being, and learning.

Bottom line, it is about *how* we do what we already are doing in classrooms and schools—teaching such subjects and classes as math, reading, science, literature, health, art, music, and physical education. It is about re-culturing schools to be developmentally supportive of how students are motivated to learn and what keeps them engaged in their learning. It is about working with, instead of against, the powerful intrinsic motivational systems (Eccles & Wigfield, 2002) that all students possess. It is about understanding neuroscience and aspects of students' developing brains enough to transfer such research into practice. It is about nurturing authentic caring relationships, maintaining appropriate high expectations, and providing meaningful opportunities for participation and contribution. It is about providing meaningful preservice and professional development opportunities for our educators that respect teachers as scholars and incorporate a deeper understanding of child development and an aptitude with such powerful tools and strategies as connecting, reflecting, and reframing. It is about asking the right questions. The question of whether we believe an individual possesses the capacity for resilience is no longer appropriate. Everyone has the capacity for resilience. The appropriate question is whether it has been tapped—and if not, what can we do to tap it?

RESILIENCE, BELIEFS, AND EDUCATION

In-depth discussions around the definitions and concepts of resilience and beliefs are provided in the subsequent chapters of this book. Yet, simply stated, resilience is a process—not a trait. It is the dynamic and negotiated process within individuals (internal) and between individuals and their environments (external) for the resources and supports to adapt and define themselves as healthy amid adversity, threat, trauma, and/or everyday stress.

Beliefs are thoughts and mindsets that affect our behaviors. They are socially constructed and often personal assumptions, judgments, generalizations, opinions, inferences, conceptions, conclusions, evaluations, and the like that we make about ourselves and the people, places, and things around us.

Resilience begins with beliefs. Nurturing resilience in an individual begins by believing that all individuals have the capacity for resilience. How does "resilience begins with beliefs" translate into our education system?

As adults working in the schools—whether as an educator, school administrator, or staff person—if we believe that a student has the capacity for resilience, then our messaging, actions, and behaviors will positively project that upon the student and awaken the resilience of that student. This in turn will contribute to that student's success in school and in life. This is one of the salient messages of this book.

WHERE DO WE BEGIN?

I have often felt and vocalized that education reform focusing solely on altering programs and curricula is often misdirected. It is imperative that we get beyond quick fixes and Band-Aid measures that have schools spending thousands of dollars investing in the newest, latest, and greatest curricula and programs in the hope that student academic success will be ensured; the achievement gap will be diminished; and teachers, researchers, administrators, policymakers, and parents will come together in a lovefest singing "Kumbaya." It takes more than a curriculum or program to sustain the level of reform we need today in our schools. If we truly want to make substantial and sustainable positive changes in our education system, we need to begin by making changes in our beliefs. That means engaging in a process, not merely purchasing a program.

Engaging in a process means dedicating preservice and professional development resources such as time, energy, and money into opportunities and safe venues where ongoing, meaningful, courageous, provocative, and authentic activities, conversations, discussions, and reflections about ourselves, our students, our communities, and our world can take place. Most educators will tell you that such professional development opportunities are few and far between.

All too often, most educators are asked to attend professional development experiences that are of the "hit and run" nature and focus more on teaching rather than learning. These are ones where a district has often purchased a curriculum and program and an afternoon or daylong session is devoted to acquainting the participants in the professional development experience with the materials and instructing them on how the materials are organized. In many cases such curricula are of a prescriptive nature, providing teachers with talking points and actual verbiage, and teachers are merely asked to follow directions for implementation. These types of professional development experiences are often ones that not only are demoralizing to teachers because the subliminal message they "hear" is that what they are currently doing is wrong or that they are not putting forth enough effort but also that if they simply follow the curriculum and program as prescribed, their students will meet with success.

Yes, educators need opportunities to acquaint themselves with curricula and programs, but they also need to know that *how* they implement those curricula and programs—especially with their tone, body language, gestures, and affect—is often what will make a difference in whether the climate and culture in the classroom and school will be the kind where optimal learning will occur.

SCHOOL CLIMATE AND CULTURE AFFECT TEACHING AND LEARNING

The climate in a school or classroom refers to the immediate feeling that one gets in an environment. Walk into the front office of a school. Do you feel welcome? Is someone there greeting you warmly and ready to assist you? Are they smiling? Walk into a classroom. Do you sense an environment where the teacher is happy to be there as well as the students? Are students on task and engaged? Is there a sense of warmth or is there a sense of tension? The climate of a school and classroom can change depending upon events. Think of a teacher who on his way to work gets into a car accident. Would that possibly affect that teacher's demeanor? How might that affect the climate in the classroom?

The culture of a classroom and school is about beliefs, attitudes, dispositions, values, and traditions, which develop over time. We can use a school garden as an example of how to distinguish between school climate and culture. Having a school garden would create a climate of pride and joy.

The creation and integration of the school garden in the curriculum reflects a school culture that values nature and real-life learning experiences. Another example that makes apparent the distinction between classroom climate and culture can be made with respect to student participation. You may walk into a classroom and see the students eager to share their opinions and thoughts. Encouraging and welcoming students to ask questions and engage in class creates a climate that is dynamic, active, and exciting. In terms of culture, the welcome participation and contributions of the students reflect a classroom culture that respects and values student participation, questions, and voice.

There is a plethora of research, literature, and resources available today that recognize the power that school climate and culture have on learning (Dary & Pickeral, 2013; Thapa, Cohen, Guffey, & Higgins-D'Alessandro, 2013). Prominent resilience researcher Michael Rutter and colleagues (Rutter, Maughan, Mortimore, Ouston, & Smith, 1979) figured out that students, age 5 through graduation, spend approximately 15,000 hours in school. Their seminal book, *Fifteen Thousand Hours*, documents their research and is often referred to as providing groundbreaking research that supports the findings that school climate and culture have an effect on student performance and success. That was in 1979. Fast-forward to 2004 . . .

Research findings such as those documented by the National Research Council and the Institute of Medicine in *Engaging Schools: Fostering High School Students' Motivation to Learn* (2004) continue to consistently support the notion that positive educational climates and cultures in classrooms and schools promote student engagement, motivation, and self-efficacy, which in turn increase student success. More specifically, resilience research and literature documented by researchers also support the monumental role school climate has in education in promoting student resilience, which in turn contributes to learning and success (Benard, 1991, 1993, 2003, 2004; Brown, D'Emidio-Caston, & Benard, 2001; Cefai, 2008; Davis, 2007; Krovetz, 1999; Schaps, 2003; Waxman, Padron, & Gray 2004).

ABOUT THIS BOOK

This book builds upon the previous work done by others in resilience research and is supported both by my own work as a researcher in the area of resilience, my policy experience as the former legislative analyst for education in the New York State Senate, and the craft knowledge I have gained as a classroom teacher for over 20 years. It explores the relationship between resilience and beliefs, posits a research-based conceptual framework that can be used for both preservice and professional development experiences for educators and administrators to influence their beliefs about student resilience in an effort to enhance student success, and provides suggestions, strategies, and support for transferring such research into practice.

One of the recurring and important messages posited by prominent resilience researchers, such as Emmy Werner and Ruth Smith (1992) and Bonnie Benard (2004), focuses on the relationship that beliefs have with resilience: Resilience begins with what one believes. As a researcher, I wanted my research in the area of resilience to begin where theirs left off. I kept thinking, "If resilience begins with beliefs—specifically beliefs in students' resilience—then what is it that needs to happen to get educators to the place of believing that all students have the capacity for resilience?" More specifically I wondered, "How could teachers' beliefs about student resilience be influenced to enhance student success?"

As a result of my exploration of this question and the continued work that I do, I contend that affecting educators' belief systems (e.g., Raths, 2001; Raths & McAninch, 2003; Richards, Gallo, & Renandya, 2001) about student resilience through well-designed and supported education preservice and professional development experiences are two concrete ways to transfer resilience research into educational practice that could promote positive school experiences and educational success for all.

One of my main goals in writing this book is to support and influence an attitude and philosophical shift in education consistent with the one so beautifully articulated by my mentor Bonnie Benard (2004)—a shift to "alter relationships, beliefs, and power opportunities so that they focus on human capacities and gifts rather than on challenges and problems" (p. 4).

WHO IS THIS BOOK FOR?

It is about time we recognize our teachers as the professionals and scholars they are. I have made a concerted effort to provide extensive references so those reading and working with this book can extend their inquiry, knowledge, and research in an area that may be of particular interest to them. It is also important for me to provide references to research because all too often individuals are quick to say that topics such as resilience and beliefs are "too soft" and not evidence driven. It is my hope that by providing such extensive references to research, educators will be equipped to rebut a comment such as this.

The contents of this book are not just to feed the head; I also hope to feed the heart and soul. Unfortunately, being a teacher is not always publicly supported, financially rewarded, or highly valued. In fact, most teachers enter the profession because they are following the call of their hearts and souls. Quotes, at times more than content, have a way of feeding our hearts and souls. Thus I have made a concerted effort to provide an extensive array of quotes, not to substitute for content, but rather to nourish the heart and soul.

I invite faculties, teachers, and administrators to use this book as a tool in their professional development to support their scholarship and understandings of research in the area of resilience, beliefs, and school climate and culture and to transfer their understandings into practice. I invite all colleges and universities to use this book in their education and administration preservice programs to impart to their students an understanding of resilience, beliefs, and the relationship between the two concepts, especially considering the powerful role that these concepts have in creating a positive educational environment. I invite boards of education and district staff to use this book as they support their teachers and administrators and commit to creating and sustaining healthy and positive teaching and learning environments in their districts. I actually invite anyone and everyone to use this book because in the end, we *all* have the honor and privilege of using our heads, hearts, and souls in making a difference in the lives of others—and it all begins with our beliefs.

ORGANIZATION OF THIS BOOK

The book begins with Chapter 1, which provides an answer to the question "What Is Resilience?" Chapter 2, "A History of Resilience," begins by explaining the distinction between a risk perspective and a resilience perspective. This chapter spends time introducing and integrating some of the seminal resilience research into the discussion. It explains how resilience is a process, not a trait, and concludes with a discussion recognizing the complexity that surrounds resilience within the research community around its definition, use, and measurement. Chapter 3, "Connecting Resilience, Beliefs, and Student Success," does just that and introduces the theory of resilience as a tool in understanding how we get from positive teacher beliefs in student resilience to positive student success. Chapter 4, "More on Beliefs," delves further into understanding why beliefs are so important in education and why is it imperative to spend time in preservice education and professional development focusing on, reflecting upon, and affecting educators' beliefs. Chapter 5, "Influencing Beliefs, Fostering Resilience, and Promoting Student Success: It's a Process, Not a Program," puts forth a conceptual framework that illustrates and discusses conceptually how resilience research gets transferred into practice through a preservice and/or professional development experience. This chapter also shares information on some of the components necessary to ensure that quality preservice and professional development experiences are being provided.

Developing a resilience perspective is often a life-changing experience for many educators. Yet sustaining a resilience perspective in education can sometimes be challenging. Chapter 6, "Sustaining Resilience in Your School, Students, and Self," feeds the heart and soul as much as it does the head. It is a collection of quotes that can be used in a variety of ways—reflected upon, taped to a wall, used as journal prompts, or just referred to every so often— to remind us about resilience, why we as educators do what we do, and not least of all, the importance of never losing focus of our own resilience. The Appendixes provide information, strategies, and tools—many of which are referenced in the text of the book—that transfer the theory from the early chapters into practice, allowing practitioners and preservice students in education the opportunity to begin answering the question that is so often asked about research and theory: "But what does it look like?"

Each chapter of this book ends with a Reflection Section. Each Reflection Section contains six questions. The first question supports the concrete understanding of a concept or idea introduced in the chapter. The second question provides an opportunity for the reader to personally connect to the concept that is being presented. Making a personal connection to a concept or idea is a potent way of developing understanding and empathy. The third question is an application question—how can you use or how have you used this knowledge in your current practice? The fourth question invites the reader to extend the concepts or ideas presented in the chapter. The fifth question asks the reader what it is that he or she may need by way of information, resources, or support to further an understanding of the concepts, ideas, tools, and/or strategies presented in the chapter. The last question asks reader to think about a question that they may still have about what they read in the chapter. This could provide a springboard for further discussion, journaling, or research.

Acknowledgments

Gratitude is one of the least articulate of the emotions,
especially when it is deep.

       —Felix Frankfurter

This book exists because of one person's belief: Brian Ellerbeck's. Brian believed in me. Brian heard about resilience from his wife, Alice, and made a point to track me down. It is only with Brian's constant encouragement and the unwavering support and hand holding that he—along with Aureliano Vazquez, Jr., and the team at Teachers College Press—provided that this book was birthed. Brian, you have been an incredible editor throughout this process and have also evolved into a dear friend.

And now for an act of futility . . .

Although I may try, I will never be able to capture and articulate in words the magnitude of support, guidance, love, and wisdom that has been bestowed upon me by beautiful Bonnie Benard. My very first meeting with Bonnie was magic. Bonnie, it was at that first meeting where you instantly—literally within minutes—opened the door to your head, heart, and soul and lovingly invited me in. Crossing that threshold, I never looked back. Needless to say, your work and radiant light have become bright beacons guiding and illuminating the paths and intersections of life and work that I now traverse. How grateful I am to have been blessed with you as a mentor, colleague, and friend.

And then there is my mom. Thank you, Mom, for giving me the gift of time to finish this book by your bedside and to witness how even in the darkest of times if we look hard enough we find the silver linings. You once again showed me in the hospital, as you always have, what it means to live life with enduring resilience, eternal optimism, and just the right amount of chutzpah.

And finally, where would I be today without all the inspirational teachers in my life? These include all the teachers who have stood in front of me while I was a student in a classroom; the teachers who have been my students in mine; the teachers who are realized through the interactions with the people who cross my path each and every day who, regardless of age, vocation, or location, enlighten and educate me about myself, others, and the world around me; and, above all, my divine teachers M. B. and M. C., who with unwavering and unconditional love and support continue to awaken me, sustaining my courage, endurance, and humility to seek what is real and true.

As I write these acknowledgments I face the fear of not being able to do complete justice in expressing my sincere gratitude and appreciation to all those who gave me permission to indulge myself in this quest. Thus, I hope the quote by Felix Frankfurter conveys what I feel in my heart and soul while I just simply and humbly say "thank you" to Chris and Ian and everyone else in my life who stood by my side and supported me through the storms and through the calm as I navigated this journey.

Introduction

Their story, yours and mine—it's what we all carry with us
on this trip we take, and we owe it to each other to respect
our stories and learn from them.

—William Carlos Williams

MY STORY

Policy

Immediately after graduating from college with a BA in psychology, I had the good fortune to work in the New York State Senate as the legislative analyst for education. I analyzed all kindergarten through high school education legislation from a programmatic perspective. My financial and legal counterparts analyzed the same legislation from their professional perspectives, respectively, after which I would most often prepare the memo that would go to the senators when they were receiving and reviewing the legislation. I also had the opportunity to work with legislators in drafting new legislation and conducting statewide hearings on provocative education topics and issues of public interest applicable and relevant to K–12 education in New York State. Much of the legislation and public hearings dealt with mandates and changes in education programs and curriculum that teachers and administrators would have to implement in their respective classrooms and schools. I was not a teacher or an education administrator. In fact, I had *never* been a teacher or an education administrator. My experience in education was as a student. Yet here I was, an instrumental player in the development of policy and legislation that would ultimately affect the quality of education in New York State. Needless to say, it was a fabulous opportunity and an exciting first job right out of college.

For my next job, I received an appointment from then New York State Governor Mario Cuomo to become special assistant to the New York State secretary of state. Once again in that capacity, I did a lot of work on education issues, policies, and legislation. For a young person in her 20s, it was another wonderful opportunity. Then it hit me.

1

As if being awakened with an epiphany, I came in to work one day and recognized that the legislation and policies I was creating for education were only as good as their implementation. I was a visionary with good intentions, yet how could I be sure that the legislation and the policies I helped create were being implemented the way I had envisioned them to be? That is when I decided to make a move from policy to practice. I wanted to teach. I realized that what really mattered in education was who was directly teaching and in contact with the students. I moved to California, went back to school, and obtained my teaching credential. As a teacher, I was astonished, and at times almost embarrassed, to think back to the legislation and policies that I worked on. I was now a practitioner in the classroom and I was able to see firsthand how some mandates and changes in education legislation and policy can negatively as well as positively affect the quality and ability not only of practitioners to teach, but also of students to learn. I recall working on a piece of legislation in the New York State Senate that was an attempt to have schools offer full-day kindergarten programs. The initial idea behind the legislation was to provide students with more time for learning. However, after being a kindergarten teacher it became abundantly clear to me that unless the full-day kindergarten program was developmentally appropriate and the teachers were well versed in child development it could possibly be more detrimental than helpful for students. Additional resources in terms of time, finances, and energy would need to be invested by educators and administrators to ensure that a full-day kindergarten program was integrated in the schools with integrity and in the best interests of all—especially in the best interests of the students.

Practice

My experience as a classroom teacher was very positive and enlightening. (I owe much of that to the fact that I had amazing colleagues who not only were incredible master teachers but also supported *my* resilience.) Administrators, parents, and colleagues often made comments about the positive, safe, and warm climate and culture in my classroom. Students were, more often than not, happy, on task, engaged, and excited about learning. They were active and involved in their own learning. They also had respect for each other and for learning. I was often asked about my classroom management program. (Others may refer to classroom management programs as discipline policies.) Parents and others would often ask me, "Where are the rules of your classroom posted?" They weren't. I didn't have rules. I didn't have a classroom management policy. I had high expectations. And the highest of all the expectations I had for everyone in the class *was* posted on the wall. That expectation was one by which all students were expected to abide. It was the Golden Rule: "Treat others as you want to be treated." I guess if push came to shove and I was forced to identify any classroom management strategies or techniques that I employed on a daily basis, I would come up with two: love and hugs.[1]

I taught in the classroom on and off for over 20 years. I had experiences teaching students from preschool to high school. Although I had different students over the years, the success of the students was always consistent and positive. Students met with success academically, socially, emotionally, and spiritually. They were motivated to learn, behaved with civility, experienced empathy toward others, and felt connected. I really thought I was not that different from other teachers. I dug deeper. I reflected upon my experience as a teacher and took a closer look into the environment I created in my classrooms to see if I could find any "constants" about my teaching. I was on my own quest and committed to try to understand and articulate what may have made others perceive my classroom environment as being different from other classrooms. I soon realized that the only thing that was truly different about me from some other teachers were my priorities. The affective aspects of my work were *always* as prominent and equal to the academic aspects; they were seamlessly woven together. Creating a classroom environment where civility, care, and community prevailed were the objectives and goals of my *being* as a teacher. A number of my classroom routines were created with this in mind.

Each morning before the students arrived, I would write a class note on the board. It was always something fun and positive. (In the early grades, it was also a great way to encourage new readers.) I was often told that the students always looked forward to coming to school to see what the message of the day would be. I also made sure that I personally greeted each and every student with a handshake and a smile every morning as he or she entered the room. I would couple this with a personal good morning phrase that included that student's name. It was often something as simple as "Good morning, Pascal." When everyone had arrived we would begin our day with a class meeting. Just as every morning started with a class meeting, every school day would end with another one. The afternoon class meeting was also a time when students would reflect and report on one nice thing that someone did for them that day and comment on how that made them feel. Upon dismissal, while the students would line up and get their belongings, I would scurry to the front door and as each child would cross the threshold, I would once again smile, shake their hands, or give a hug, and this time I would say at least one positive thing to them that I noticed about their day. I did this when I taught kindergarten as well as when I taught high school.

---

1. In today's world, where we need to be cognizant of "inappropriate touch," I also use the term "hugs" to capture actions and behaviors that authentically and sincerely express love and caring to students such as empathetic eyes, tender smiles, gentle pats on the back, responsive side-by-side hugs, and warm handshakes.

My practical experience in teaching, coupled with my personal experiences as a student, shaped and supported the development of my "intuitive" theory: Students learn best in environments that not only create a sense of community but also promote and model authentic civility, care, and love. I continued to share my theory with others who asked me what I would do to improve the quality of education today. Holding strong to my conviction that teaching and learning begin in the heart, not the head, my advice was always simple: Love and hug the kids.

Dispensing this advice seemed a bit too simplistic and "soft" for some. As a result, my personal mission and goal were established; I wanted to be heard. It was then that I decided to begin my journey toward a doctorate so I could be perceived and received as being more credible when I tell educators and stakeholders in education to "love and hug their kids."

Research

My quest to articulate and support my own experiential and intuitive theories about education led to the discovery of the concept, resilience: the ability to bounce back in the face of adversity or stress. As a doctoral student I latched on to the concept of resilience. It resonated with me as a teacher, as a student, and as a human being. I needed to know more.

Early in my research, I read a theory about resilience that had been suggested and applied in education. In Bonnie Benard's seminal work, *Resiliency: What We Have Learned* (2004), a theory of resilience was posited that identified the relationship between student needs, elements in an environment, individual strengths, and student success. The theory articulated that three elements needed to be present in an environment, in this specific context a classroom, so that students, especially those from high-risk environments, could "bounce back" from adversity, reduce health risks, and be successful as students. The three elements were consistent with my practices of providing love and hugs, expecting the students to follow the Golden Rule, and engaging kids in their own learning—only now, instead of "elements," they were called "protective factors" and respectively identified by the more scholarly accepted terms: providing authentic caring relationships, maintaining high expectations, and providing meaningful opportunities for student participation and contribution.

Putting It All Together

My array of experiential knowledge in education equipped me with the ability not only to speak and understand the language of education policy, practice, and research but also to witness and evaluate their real educational and societal implications. That, coupled with a doctorate in educational leadership, would perhaps make people more inclined not just to hear me but maybe they would listen. Today when I am asked by others, "Why did you get your doctorate?" my answer is simple: "With some letters behind my name, maybe now people will listen to me when I tell them to love and hug their students."

TODAY'S STORY

Although schools can make structural changes, until schools address underlying beliefs and perceptions, the educational system is failing our youth and society.

—Patrice De La Ossa, "Hear My Voice"

Individuals and stakeholders with an interest in increasing the educational success of all students can benefit by developing a deeper understanding of resilience and an enhanced awareness regarding the role that one's beliefs have in shaping such a concept. This is vitally important to educators and adults working in the schools because their beliefs about student resilience will translate into messages, actions, and behaviors that will enhance or impede their students' success and achievement in education and in life.

Very simply stated, resilience is one's ability to spring back from adversity or stress. Resilience research in education focuses on healthy development and successful learning, especially with young people facing difficult life challenges in their homes, schools, and communities. Beliefs are thoughts and mindsets that affect our behaviors. They are socially constructed and often personal assumptions, judgments, generalizations, opinions, inferences, conceptions, conclusions, evaluations, and the like that we make about ourselves and the people, places, and things around us. My research, work, and interest in education continues to explore the relationship between the two constructs: resilience and beliefs.

Resilience research is critical to education. The National Research Council and the Institute of Medicine (2004) and a number of prominent researchers such as Carol Dweck (2006), Nel Noddings (2003), Michael Rutter (1979), and Eric Schaps (2000) have already shown through their work that motivation, learning, and the achievement gap are just some areas of education where resilience research has vital implications for practice and policy. Their data indicate that when classroom environments and schools consistently foster caring relationships, maintain high expectations for all students, and provide opportunities for students to participate and contribute, students from these nurturing environments are more successful in school.

Education research on teacher beliefs (e.g., Fullan, 2008; Guskey, 1986; Jackson, 2011; Jussim, 1986; Kagan, 1992; Pajares, 1992, 1993; Yero, 2002) focuses on understanding how teacher beliefs affect and influence teacher practices and student outcomes. Teacher differences in attitudes and beliefs can negatively or positively affect student success. Teacher attitudes and beliefs about students can differ based upon things such as a student's race, ethnicity, social class, disability, and gender.

Nancy Love (2000), in her book *Using Data/Getting Results: Collaborative Inquiry for School Based Mathematics and Science Reform*, recognizes that "examining belief systems takes courage and conviction." She also asserts that engaging in an examination of belief systems and how they influence education and student outcomes is the "true measure of our 'will to educate all children,' for it is only by breaking the silence about racism, classism, and sexism that we can begin to break their grip on our society and our schools" (p. 7).

One of the recurring messages posited by such prominent resilience researchers as Emmy Werner, Ruth Smith, and Bonnie Benard focuses on the relationship that beliefs have with resilience: Resilience begins with beliefs. As educators, if we believe that a student has the capacity for resilience, then our messaging, actions, and behaviors will positively project that upon the student and that student will awaken his or her resilience and meet with success in school and in life.

In the conclusion of her seminal book, *Resiliency: What We Have Learned*, Benard (2004) asks about the steps ahead in the work of resilience and youth development: "What must we provide for youth, and for those who work with them? How can we have the most effect? And what challenges must we address?" She suggests "we need to begin with belief in the innate resilience of every human being" (p. 113).

Situating this within the context of education, I contend that educators who possess an understanding of resilience and the belief that student resilience is a process that can be tapped within each student can create educational environments that make a positive contribution to increasing student success. Applied research and craft knowledge support this. Practitioners in education who embrace an intuitive theory of student resilience, who without being prompted or taught create classroom climates and school cultures where high expectations are held, caring relationships are fostered, and opportunities for student engagement are provided and encouraged, often experience positive academic and social student outcomes, which in turn continue to positively influence and reinforce teacher beliefs about student resilience. These teachers, administrators, and staff, even without formal knowledge of resilience theory in education, continue to create such classroom climates and school cultures because of one of two reasons. One, they instinctively attribute the classroom and school climate and culture as variables in promoting and sustaining positive student success. Two, upon reflection they found that when they engaged in specific practices and behaviors that they can attribute to supporting a positive classroom and school environment (such as being culturally responsive, sustaining high expectations, honoring each student's unique strengths, and practicing equity and inclusion), students affectively and cognitively responded in positive ways. This encouraged such teachers to continue and embrace the specific practices and behaviors that they were implementing in their classrooms. As in this case, the relationship between positive classroom and school climate and culture and the increase in students' resilience and success becomes part of that practitioner's craft knowledge and beliefs—knowledge and beliefs about best practices that are accumulated and reinforced from continued experiences.

Although much of the research focusing on beliefs and practices does so in the context of beliefs influencing practices, researchers in education such as Thomas Guskey (1986) and Michael Fullan (2008) agree that "beliefs and practices" can often present the same dilemma as the "Which came first, the chicken or the egg?" conundrum and support the idea, as I do, that it can go both ways: Beliefs can influence behaviors *and* behaviors can, in fact, influence beliefs. Perhaps there is a teacher who just does not believe that girls are as competent in math as are boys and as a result does not call on girls who have their hands raised to answer many questions. As a result, the girls don't seem to be as engaged as the boys in class. That teacher complains about the girls not being engaged in class to his colleagues. One of his colleagues has a thought that maybe it is not the girls who aren't engaged but rather the teacher whose behaviors are in the way. That colleague respectfully encourages the teacher to see what might happen if he were to just try to be more aware of calling on a girl more often in class. The next day the teacher does just that and calls on more girls than he has in the past. They seem to positively respond. The teacher attributes the girls' positive engagement and response to just a fluke but continues to call on more girls over the next few days of class—just to see what happens. After a week of making more of a concerted effort to call on girls the teacher recognizes that as a group, the girls have, in fact, become more engaged and eager to respond. The teacher then takes time to earnestly reflect and begins to humbly recognize and courageously admit that his long-held belief that girls were not as competent as boys in math contributed to his behavior of not calling on the girls as much in class. With his new behavior, and witnessing firsthand the positive results of his behavior, he no longer holds to a former belief he once had.

In the end, perhaps the most important point, even above directionality, is to recognize that a relationship between educators' beliefs, practices, and ultimately student outcomes exists and that focusing efforts on affecting beliefs, dispositions, and attitudes—sources that greatly influence human behavior—can be a critical component in helping us create and sustain classroom and school climates and cultures that foster student success. Gary Fenstermacher (1979), a professor of education at the School of Education at the University of Michigan, in an article on teacher effectiveness identified beliefs to eventually become the "single most important construct in educational research" (p. 329).

Research already demonstrates the role that resilience plays in students' success and the role that teachers' beliefs play in creating classroom environments that foster student resilience. A review of the literature and research that discuss teacher beliefs in the context of education reveals support for the claim that preservice education and professional development can influence teacher beliefs and practices in a number of ways (Fang, 1996; Hollingsworth, 1989). Research done by Lawrence and Tatum (1997) demonstrated that a well-crafted staff development program could influence teachers' beliefs and attitudes about race and ethnicity. Brownell and Pajares (1996), through their work with educators of students with diverse learning and behavioral needs, recognized "the importance of creating educational experiences and supports that foster a general education teacher's efficacy beliefs and success in teaching students with diverse learning and behavioral needs" (p. 16). Richardson and colleagues (Richardson, Anders, Tidwell, & Lloyd, 1991) concluded from their research about the relationship between teachers' beliefs and practices in reading comprehension that positive student outcomes can be enhanced when well-crafted staff development programs incorporate knowledge about educators' beliefs and understandings.

This is very powerful, especially since a practitioner's beliefs and perceptions about a particular student or family can be developed without regard to prior knowledge about, or experience with, that student or family. Students' perceptions and beliefs of their own abilities and capacity for learning can positively or negatively be affected, respectively, by a teacher's perceptions and beliefs.

An important aspect of how beliefs influence practices and outcomes is found in sociologist Robert K. Merton's (1968) work about the phenomenon known as the self-fulfilling prophecy and Harvard psychologist Robert Rosenthal and school principal Lenore Jacobson's (Rosenthal & Jacobson, 1968) work around the Pygmalion effect, a form of the self-fulfilling prophecy. The "self-fulfilling prophecy" refers to an individual's self-efficacy, perception, belief, and manifestation of his/her own abilities and capacity for learning and change, which can positively or negatively be influenced by others' perceptions, expectations, and beliefs—regardless of whether such beliefs are correct or incorrect. The Pygmalion effect, named after a play by George Bernard Shaw, was based upon the experiment conducted by

Rosenthal and Jacobson that specifically applied the self-fulfilling prophecy in the context of education. With respect to the Pygmalion effect, executive editor of *The National Teaching and Learning Forum* James Rhem (1999), in an article about Rosenthal and Jacobson's book, *Pygmalion in the Classroom*, wrote, "Simply put, when teachers expect students to do well and show intellectual growth, they do; when teachers do not have such expectations, performance and growth are not so encouraged and may in fact be discouraged in a variety of ways" (p. 1).

The following is an example of the self-fulfilling prophecy in action: A high school student continually hears from his teachers and parents that he is lazy and hopeless. The student begins to believe what he repeatedly hears from others and concludes to himself that he is lazy, unmotivated, hopeless, and a failure. Such thoughts hinder the student's motivation to want to work harder or engage further in studying or completing tasks and homework assignments. The student acts in ways that are consistent with the expectations maintained and communicated by his teachers and parents. The student fails. The student reflects on the situation by concluding that his teachers and parents were right: "I am lazy, hopeless, and a failure." This is how a student could potentially get stuck with a self-destructive mindset.

Stanford University researcher Carol Dweck (2006), in her widely acclaimed book, *Mindset: The New Psychology of Success*, introduces and discusses the concept and power of mindsets. She distinguishes between a fixed mindset and a growth mindset. Simply stated, people with a fixed mindset believe their traits and abilities, such as personality, intelligence, and talents, are "what they are" and cannot be changed. Thus they resign themselves to accepting whatever outcomes occur as a result of their existing efforts on a task. On the other hand, people with a growth mindset believe that their traits and abilities are malleable and can be cultivated through their own efforts. This translates into individuals who reach higher for themselves and embrace a "can-do" attitude around tasks. Individuals with a growth mindset are often optimistic and persistent as they welcome the challenge of putting forth additional effort to reach higher for themselves. Dweck's book shares how our mindsets affect our lives and the way we engage in activities—from business, to love, to relationships, to learning. Prior to providing a comprehensive discussion about mindsets, she succinctly articulates what mindsets are: "Mindsets are just beliefs. They're powerful beliefs, but they're something in your mind, and you can change your mind" (p. 16).

So often, the negative repercussions from the self-fulfilling prophecy, the Pygmalion effect, and having a fixed mindset work in detrimental ways when we fail to take the time to hear and understand each other's stories. Prominent educator and author Paula Lawrence Wehmiller (1992) impresses upon us the detrimental disservice that is done when we don't know each other's stories:

When there are walls of ignorance between people, where we don't know each
other's stories, we substitute our own myth about who that person is. When we
are operating with only a myth, none of that person's truth will ever be known
to us, and we will injure them—mostly without ever meaning to. What assumption did you make because she is a woman? What assumption did you make
because she is black? What myths were built around the neighborhood listed on
the application? What myths were built around the employment of the father
or the absence of the mother? What story did we tell ourselves in the absence of
knowing this person's real story? (p. 380)

All beliefs, whether they are those we have of others or ones we have
of ourselves, are extraordinarily powerful. Beliefs are forces to be reckoned with and should be given the respect and attention that they de-
serve—especially beliefs about resilience. Hence, my motivation in writing
this book.

CREATING THE BRIDGE FROM RESEARCH TO PRACTICE

This book provides readers with the opportunity to bridge research to practice. Research in the area of resilience exists. Research in the area of beliefs exists. A theoretical assumption about the relationship between beliefs
and resilience exists: Resilience begins with beliefs. Although this theoretical assumption exists, concrete questions need to be answered to bridge
the theory with the practice. These questions include the following: How
is resilience defined? If resilience begins with beliefs—specifically beliefs in
students' resilience—then what is it that needs to happen to get educators
to that place of believing that all students have the capacity for resilience?
How can teachers' beliefs about student resilience be influenced to enhance
student success? What are some beliefs, strategies, and tools that educators
and administrators can embrace in their classrooms, schools, and districts
to tap, support, and sustain resilience in their students?
    Much of this book draws upon the research I did for my dissertation,
*Tell Me a Story: Influencing Educators' Beliefs about Student Resilience in
an Effort to Enhance Student Success* (Truebridge, 2010), which included
the development and facilitation of a professional development experience
to explore its effectiveness in influencing teachers' and staffs' beliefs about
student resilience. The specific goal of the professional development experience was to create a venue where education practitioners could learn
about the concept and theory of resilience and reflect upon their beliefs
to enhance their effectiveness in tapping, supporting, and increasing their
students' resilience and hence success in school. The question that drove

my work was, How does a professional development program on the concept of student resilience affect the pedagogical beliefs and practices of practitioners in education? However, I wanted my research question to explore whether the concept of beliefs and practices emerged from the participants themselves as they engaged in the professional development process. I did not want to direct, bias, or limit the participants' focus, so I ultimately crafted the research question to be, How do educators respond to a professional development program regarding the concept of resilience? Sure enough, recognizing and reflecting upon how beliefs affect practices evolved from the participants in the professional development themselves and became a major focus and component in the professional development experience.

What Is Resilience?

Researchers spend a lot of time finding just the right definition of resilience. Chapter 2 provides an in-depth discussion that covers the history of resilience, the complexity of the definition, and the arguments that have been made to defend the construct. Yet for the purpose of providing a working definition for carrying the current discussion forward in this book, I have combined and built upon the work of other resilience researchers such as Michael Rutter, Ann Masten, Suniya Luthar, Bonnie Benard, and Michael Ungar and offer the definition of resilience as the dynamic and negotiated process within individuals (internal) and between individuals and their environments (external) for the resources and supports to adapt and define themselves as healthy amid adversity, threat, trauma, and/or everyday stress. The internal process consists of tapping into one's personal strengths, attributes, past experiences, etc. The external process involves being surrounded by school, family, and community resources, supports, and services such as counselors, community-based organizations, financial assistance, etc. Another way to define resilience is to simply say that resilience is the self-righting and transcending capacity within all youth, adults, organizations, and communities to spring back, rebound, and

resiliencia def.

successfully adapt in the face of trauma, adversity, and/or everyday stress. An even more simplistic definition would be to say that resilience is the ability to spring back from adversity. One of the most important things to understand around the concept of resilience that is inherent in all the definitions is that resilience is a process, not a trait.

{cont.

WHY IS AN UNDERSTANDING OF RESILIENCE IMPORTANT TO EDUCATORS?

You would have to look long and hard to find someone who would argue with the statement that schools and classrooms are often a place of adversity and stress for both students and educators. You would also have a hard time arguing that our beliefs do not influence our actions.

The following scenario in education poignantly conveys the dangers and repercussions of wrongly perceiving resilience as a trait and not understanding that our beliefs affect our behaviors.

Let's say you are a 6th-grade teacher and it is the morning of the first day of school. You ask all your students to line up against the wall. You then slowly walk to the first person in line and point at her declaring, "Becky, you're resilient. Please take a giant step forward." Then you proceed to slowly work your way down the line and as you do, you point to each student and identify whether he or she is resilient or not. "Linda, you're resilient. Please step forward." "Don, you're resilient. Step forward." "Merwan, you're resilient. You too can take a step forward." Then you hesitate when you arrive at Debby, and state loud enough for all to hear, "Debby, you're *not* resilient. Please stay back—against the wall." You then continue on: "Julio, you're resilient. Step forward." "Isabel, you're resilient. You can step forward." "Oops, Cameron. Sorry, but you're *not* resilient. Please stay there against the wall."

After going through the whole class of 27 students, you end up identifying the majority of your students as resilient. However, seven of them receive the label "not resilient." Those seven are now standing against the wall one giant step behind the other 20 you just labeled "resilient." That probably took 10 minutes, but the repercussions of what you did in those 10 minutes will be felt by those students for a lifetime.

By doing what you just did, you have sent a signal to the students and to yourself. The signal you have sent to the majority of your students is that they can look forward to an exciting year of caring, high expectations, and opportunities to participate in and contribute to a host of activities and discussions. But what about the other seven? What signal did you send to them? The signal they received was that they are broken—no matter what they do, they will not meet with success; no matter how hard they try or whatever opportunities are made available to them, they still will not meet with success. The signal that you have sent to yourself is that they are broken—these seven students may never be able to spring back from whatever adversity you perceive they are living amid now or have encountered in their past. Furthermore, you may conclude that to continue investing your time and energy in working with these students is a waste of your time. No matter how hard you or they try, or whatever attempts you or they make, the students' destiny has already been determined and sealed—they are *not* resilient.

This scenario is highly exaggerated and I can hardly imagine that anyone would deliberately and blatantly engage in such an activity. Yet this type of activity often happens subliminally when we engage in some common educational practices. It happens in the fall as some teachers read the cumulative files of their incoming students. It happens as teachers share conversations in the staff room. It happens as teachers read a child's name and then reflect upon his/her sibling, parents, or family. So what? The big "so what" is that what you believe about these students will most likely be reflected in your behaviors and actions in the classroom.

Let's go back to the seven students in the scenario who were identified and labeled "not resilient." How might a teacher's behavior be affected—what might this look like? As the teacher, you might not give these seven students as much attention as you would the other students; you might not care as much about how your time was spent working with them. Or perhaps you find that you don't expect as much from your seven "*not* resilient" students as you do from the others you labeled "resilient." Perhaps, and truly without consciously knowing, you may not call on them as much to contribute to class discussions or select them as often to participate in activities.

Yes, it is true; our beliefs affect our behaviors. A teacher or school administrator's beliefs will affect his or her behavior, which in turn will affect a student. Further, education research and educators' stories confirm that the scenario as described above, where a teacher's behavior has been influenced by belief in the capacity of a student, although not intentional and not so exaggerated, plays out all across schools and classrooms camouflaged in a variety of ways.

IMPORTANT INSIGHTS FROM RESILIENCE RESEARCH

Regardless of how one defines resilience—and there are a number of variations of the definition that one can find in the literature and research—the following major messages and contributions from resilience research relay important information that should be understood and embraced by all individuals with an interest in education. They are as follows:

1. Resilience is a process, not a trait. It is a dynamic and negotiated process within individuals (internal) and between individuals and their environments (external) for the resources and supports to adapt and define themselves as healthy amid adversity, threat, trauma, and/or everyday stress.
2. All people have the capacity for resilience. The question isn't whether or not one has resilience, but rather whether or not it has been tapped.
3. Most individuals *do* make it despite exposure to severe risk. Consistent with resilience research (Werner & Smith, 1992), at least 50%, and usually closer to 70%, of children and youth from high-risk environments overcome adversity and achieve good developmental outcomes.
4. Coming from a risk environment does not determine individual outcomes. A child of color born into poverty to a single mother who is abusing drugs is not destined to become a gang member.
5. Bad behavior does not equate with being a bad person. Just because a student may display inappropriate behavior, such as hitting another student or cheating on an assignment, that doesn't make the student a bad person. What the student did was display poor judgment and as a result, the student needs to be responsible for those actions. However, a person who displays bad judgment is not "forever" a bad person.
6. One person can make a difference in the life of another person. One person—like a teacher, relative, or friend—can say something to us one day or believe in us in a way that can change our lives forever.
7. Challenging life experiences and events can be opportunities for growth, development, and change. Quite often our perseverance through tough times builds our confidence and makes us stronger.
8. Many personal strengths (e.g., cognitive, social, emotional, moral/spiritual) are associated with resilience. These personal strengths not only foster resilience, but also manifest as outcomes of resilience.
9. Three major environmental protective factors (developmental supports and opportunities) can be identified that mitigate adversities and nourish the personal strengths associated with resilience:
    a. Caring relationships—provide a sense of connectedness and belonging; demonstrate "being there"; exude compassion and trust.
    b. High expectations—convey a focus on strengths; stabilize routines; offer positive messaging in the belief of others as one is both challenged and supported at the same time.

    c. Opportunities to participate and contribute—contribute to personal power, inclusion, and self-efficacy; awaken the power and gifts of "service"; and instill responsibility, voice, and choice.

10. As a practitioner, it is *how* you do *what* you do that counts. For instance, as a teacher you can teach a difficult concept while being open to students' questions and supporting them for their persistence and determination in their attempt to understand a difficult concept, or you can inhibit, embarrass, or shame them for asking questions during a lesson.

11. To help others, you need to help yourself; resilience is a parallel process. It's the "oxygen mask on an airplane" analogy—in order for you to be able to help someone else, you first have to help yourself. Take care of the caretaker. You always need to find ways to support your own resilience while you are supporting the resilience of others.

12. Resilience begins with beliefs. Our beliefs influence our actions. If you don't believe in the capacity of all individuals to have resilience, then you run the risk of giving up on them.

RESILIENCE: THE WORD OF THE DAY

Although resilience is not a new concept, the word *resilience* has become a familiar and popular word in today's lexicon. That is good because it is an important concept not only as it relates to education but also as it relates to life—everyone's life. Yet at the same time it presents a challenge. One reason why I take the liberty to say it presents a challenge is that often when a word becomes popular it gets thrown around, overused, abused, and misused. When a word reaches such a point of saturation in our vocabulary, there is often an assumption made that everyone using the word understands the meaning or concept behind the word.

Another concern I have about the word *resilience* becoming so popular is that we have seen how the pendulum continually swings in education. Often when a word becomes a "buzzword" it can stick for a while but then after some time, it gets old and feels passé. When this happens stakeholders in education have a tendency to create new words and attach them to former concepts—just for the simple sake of change. Change is good. But in situations where change is made just for the sake of change, we have to ask ourselves whose interests are being served. When some researchers, experts, politicians, and textbook and curriculum publishers attach new words and create new programs and materials to things that "don't need to be fixed," it often leads to good news for them—for doing such can benefit, bolster, and inflate CVs, egos, and financial resources. Yet it wreaks havoc on practitioners who often are asked to invest already depleted resources, such as time and money, into *new* programs, curricula, and materials.

The good news about the concept of resilience is that teachers and administrators do not need to purchase a new program or curriculum telling them how to create a school climate or culture where student resilience is tapped and nurtured. Integrating the concept of resilience into an educator's practice is not done with a program. It is done by engaging in a process—a process that consists of having quality time with colleagues to know and understand the concept of resilience from a scholarly perspective and then, with their professional knowledge and wisdom of being in the trenches, engage in the process of transferring such information into practice. Through my work in the schools I have seen firsthand how teachers and administrators have benefited and appreciated having dedicated and quality time with their colleagues and their educational community to explore understandings, situations, strategies, and tools within the context of resilience. This includes providing a safe environment for them to engage in a process where they can reflect upon their beliefs, especially how they pertain to student resilience. Appendix B provides a Possible/Suggested Format for a Preservice/ Professional Development Experience that reinforces the understanding that resilience begins with beliefs.

Reflection Section

1. Some of the main concepts, ideas, tools, and/or strategies I learned from this chapter include _____.

2. A personal experience that allows me to relate to the concepts, ideas, tools, and/or strategies presented in the chapter occurred _____.

3. An example of how I have used or will use the concepts, ideas, tools, and/or strategies presented in the chapter in my current practice is _____.

4. In my future practice I would like to build upon the concepts, ideas, tools, and/or strategies presented in the chapter by _____.

5. Ways in which I may need more information, resources, or support to further an understanding or implementation of the concepts, ideas, tools, and/or strategies presented in the chapter are _____.

6. A question I still have about the concepts, ideas, tools, and/or strategies presented in the chapter is _____.

A History of Resilience

What began as a quest to understand the extraordinary has revealed the power of the ordinary. Resilience does not come from rare and special qualities, but from the everyday magic of the ordinary, normative human resources in the minds, brains, and bodies of children, in their families and relationships, and in their communities.

—Ann Masten, *Ordinary Magic*

Adversity has the effect of eliciting talents, which in prosperous circumstances would have lain dormant.

—Horace

Resilience is not a new concept. Resilience research emerged over 50 years ago as researchers began asking the question, Why do some children who are exposed to high-risk environments successfully adapt while others do not (Garmezy, 1987; Garmezy & Masten, 1986; Garmezy & Rutter, 1983; Lester, Masten, & McEwen, 2006; Rutter, 1979; Werner & Smith, 1992)? The vast body of resilience research has provided the foundation of and contributed to many popular movements, such as asset development, positive youth development, strengths-based practice, and positive psychology.

FROM RISK TO RESILIENCE

The study of resilience has contributed to the dramatic shift in the fields of education, human development, prevention, and intervention. It is a shift from viewing the world and individuals through traditional problem-based, deficit, pathology models to positive, strengths-based, protective, and preventive models. The shift comes from an increasing body of research in neuroscience, psychology, social work, and education that recognizes resilience not only internally in individuals but also externally in families, communities, and wider social environments. Furthermore, the study of resilience has expanded from an early focus on the individual to a broader, more inclusive focus that situates risk not in children, but rather in a variety of socioecologic systems, institutions, and harmful public and social policies (Bronfenbrenner, 1979; D. M. Davis, 2007; Hall & Hord, 2006).

The example in the Preface, of a student who comes from an abusive home, illustrates how a teacher can possess a choice of whether to view a situation through a risk-based lens or a resilience lens. There are some major negative repercussions for teachers who maintain a risk-based deficit perspective. For one, it does not provide an answer to what works. Second, it tends to label students according to their problems. Third, it leads to a loss of belief in students' capacity and potential. All three of the aforementioned repercussions ultimately lead to a sense of hopelessness on the part of the teacher that also gets transferred to the students themselves.

RESILIENCE AS A PROCESS

Although today resilience is widely understood as a process—the interaction of resources and supports within an individual and external to the individual such as family, school, community, and peer group—it hasn't always been clearly defined or understood as such. Early resilience studies focused on the personal qualities of resilient children. As a result, resilience was seen by many to be a trait. Resilience researcher Suniya Luthar and colleagues (Luthar, Cicchetti, & Becker, 2000a) discuss the negative repercussions that can result from this interpretation. To say that resilience is a trait is in essence to say "that some individuals simply do not 'have what it takes' to overcome adversity" (p. 546). This perspective was not embraced or universally demonstrated in resilience research. Once again, resilience is a process, not a trait.

SOME IMPORTANT UNDERSTANDINGS EMBEDDED IN THE CONSTRUCT OF RESILIENCE

Valuing and treating educators as professionals and scholars means providing enough research so as not to bog educators down but rather to provide them with a deeper understanding of a concept—such as resilience—so that they can thoughtfully explore, develop, and sustain ways to positively transfer research into practice. I put forth the following four understandings about resilience with this in mind.

Protective Processes

Protective processes, like protective factors, buffer and mitigate risk and adversity. They refer to the complex interactions that occur between an individual and one's family, school, community, peer group, and other external systems. A caring teacher would be a protective factor for a student. The overt (e.g., behavioral) and underlying (e.g., cognitive and emotional) dynamics, interactions, and responses that occur between that teacher and that student would be a protective process. A protective process refers to something that happens—it is active.

A 1987 paper by Michael Rutter went beyond protective "factors" and identified protective "processes" as an important area of focus in resilience research. Rutter identified the work in resilience as a quest "to ask *why* and *how* some individuals manage to maintain high self-esteem and self-efficacy in spite of facing the same adversities that lead other people to give up and lose hope. The search is not for broadly defined protective factors, but rather, for the developmental and situational mechanisms involved in protective processes" (pp. 316–317). Resilience researcher Suniya Luthar (2006) notes that as the study in resilience continued to grow in the 1980s and 1990s so did the complexities. Additional features of resilience spawned new questions. One was the "locus" of resilience. The other was the issue of time. Another included the issues of perspective, culture, power, and privilege.

Locus of Resilience

The locus of resilience refers to whether resilience is internally or externally generated. That is, does it come from within a person or from his or her environment? As the study of resilience progressed, resilience moved beyond the scope of just recognizing *internal* personal traits, strengths, and assets that contributed to the protective process and included the interaction of factors *external* to the individual—family, school, community, peer group, and other external systems.

Time

Time became another feature that generated new questions in resilience research. Findings recognized that resilience is an adaptive process that can fluctuate depending upon changing life circumstances and context. People may be able to tap their resilience in the face of one adversity, such as the death of a friend, but not in the death of a parent. A person may be able to tap his or her own resilience in the face of one natural disaster such as a tornado, but not in another such as a flood. Furthermore, a person may be able to tap resilience through a challenging experience but not at another time when confronted with the same challenging experience. Resilience is neither linear nor static.

Perspective, Culture, Power, and Privilege

How a person perceives an experience plays an important role in individual variability with resilience. A tremendous disservice is done to the field of resilience when the identification of socially or culturally normative and appropriate behaviors are upheld as the litmus test of resilience. What may be considered a manifestation of resilience to one population, culture, or group may be undesirable to another. As resilience researcher Michael Ungar (2004) states, "Each localized discourse that defines a group's concept of resilience is privileged, more or less depending on the power of those who articulate it" (p. 345).

Take the example of a teen who chooses to be in a gang. By most normative social standards, this behavior would be labeled as being undesirable, if not blatantly deviant. I offer an alternative perspective. What if the teen felt vulnerable and targeted for some unconscionable consequence because he or she was *not* in a gang? In this case, the teen may suggest that he or she became a part of a gang in order to stay alive on the streets. Was that individual demonstrating resilience?

Although there now is agreement in the field that resilience is a process rather than a trait, literature still gets misinterpreted. Because resiliency and resilient were often misinterpreted to refer to traits, resilience researcher Ann Masten (1994) suggests that the term *resilience*—not *resiliency*—be used when referring to the process of positive adaptation in the face of adversity.

A COMPLEX DEFINITION

The research community has yet to come up with a truly consistent definition of resilience—a fact that makes the study and evaluation of resilience challenging yet exciting. As with most definitions of resilience, the concept is made up of two other concepts: adversity and adaptation. For example, resilience researcher Suniya Luthar and colleagues (Luthar et al., 2000a) refer to resilience as "a dynamic process encompassing positive adaptation within the context of significant adversity" (p. 543). What is considered "significant" adversity? Is "positive" adaptation normative adaptation? Is it returning to the level of adaptation that an individual exhibited prior to an adversity or is it exceeding that level of adaptation? Furthermore, Luthar (2006) identifies the construct of resilience as a phenomenon that "is never directly measured, but rather is indirectly inferred based on evidence of the two subsumed constructs" (p. 742). Thus, resilience as a construct—its definition, application, and assessment—is complicated because of having to define, operationalize, and assess the two constructs of adversity and adaptation.

Positive adaptation has been operationalized in a variety of ways, including the identification of successfully manifesting specific social competences, stage-salient developmental tasks, and/or school-based markers that include, but are not limited to, academic competencies. Further discrepancies and complications in the study of resilience exist because positive adaptation begs the question, Does that mean *better than expected* outcomes or positive outcomes in spite of adversity?

Significant is often the word used to describe the type of adversity reflected in definitions and discussions related to resilience. I continue to question the use of this adjective. In most deficit models, significant adversity, or risk, has often been operationalized by identifying individuals' exposure to high-risk environments and then quantifying the statistical probabilities of maladjustment. Some high-risk environments identified include ones where poverty, violence, substance abuse/addiction, and/or parental depression are prevalent. Yet what is considered a high-risk environment or "significant" adversity by one person might not be seen as one through the eyes of someone else. For instance, more stakeholders in education are beginning to recognize affluent communities—communities once believed to "have it all"—as being a high-risk environment for some (Luthar, Barkin, & Crossman, in press). This was made evident by many of the issues and circumstances presented in the documentary film *Race to Nowhere* (Abeles, 2009), which highlighted a number of affluent communities where students and parents were driven to unhealthy levels of demonstrating excellence, achievement, and performance by the high grades, AP classes, first-place trophies, and extracurricular activities they could amass. Adding to the complexity of significant adversity, resilience research finds that significant adversity is not always easily defined by the identification of one high-risk variable.

A number of resilience studies (Gutman, Sameroff, & Cole, 2003; Rutter, 1979; Sameroff, Gutman, & Peck, 2003) have focused on how multiple and cumulative high-risk environmental factors affect outcomes. It is also important to remember that resilience can situate itself in different contexts. Three types of resilience that are often discussed are as follows:

1. Overcoming the Odds—achieving positive outcomes despite a high risk for poor outcomes. An example of this would be a teen mother who successfully graduates high school.
2. Sustained Competence Under Stress—ability to cope with a chronic, high level of stress. An example of this would be a student who

lives in a chronically abusive home and continues to be successful in school.

3. Recovery from Trauma—ability to maintain or return to a high level of functioning after an intensely stressful or damaging event. An example of this would be a student who continues to be successful in school after a parent has committed suicide.

It is evident that the multitude of ways to identify and categorize adaptation and adversity as well as the contexts in which resilience is discussed continue to complicate the study of resilience.

DEFENDING THE CONSTRUCT OF RESILIENCE

Leaders in resilience research often find themselves writing to respond to colleagues in the scientific and scholarly community who question the concept of resilience, the rigor regarding the theory of resilience, and the validity of research on resilience (Luthar et al., 2000a, 2000b). Resilience researcher Michael Rutter (2006) acknowledges, "Whenever a new term becomes fashionable, it is always necessary to consider whether it is simply a new way of repackaging old material or whether it introduces some new perspective" (p. 3). Rutter provides a thorough discussion in response to the question of how resilience differs from the concepts of risk and protection. In addressing this question, Rutter notes that "resilience requires the prior study of risk and protection but adds a different new dimension" (p. 3).

The study of risk and protection begins with an assumption that risk and protective factors affect everyone relatively, to the same degree (Rutter, 2006). The outcome differences that are measurable are a result of how risks and protective factors balance each other. This differs from resilience. Rutter explains:

> Resilience starts with a recognition of the huge individual variation in people's responses to the same experiences, and considers outcomes with the assumption that an understanding of the mechanisms underlying that variation will cast light on the causal processes and, by doing so, will have implications for intervention strategies with respect to both prevention and treatment. (p. 3)

The complexity of dynamic interactions and the fact that individuals respond in different ways and in different degrees to similar experiences support the study of resilience. Resilience does not reside as a trait in a person or as a single attribute in an environment, but rather as a neurological as well as psychological process and interaction between an individual and the environment (Lerner, 2006).

Research consistently supports and corroborates, respectively, that the three protective factors—caring relationships, high expectations, and meaningful opportunities to participate and contribute—are protective factors associated with resilience in students. They have made it onto what some researchers refer to as the "short list"—protective factors consistently corroborated by research in the field of resilience (Glantz & Johnson, 1999). Protective factors often work together. Furthermore some protective factors have been identified to substitute for others. For instance, one caring adult in a school has often been identified to be an important substitute for students who may not have a caring parent in their home life. The power of one caring adult cannot be underestimated. This finding has tremendous implications for how adults in schools not only are prepared before working in the schools but also are provided with professional development once in the schools.

As mentioned, resilience research recognizes that protective factors become integrated in a dynamic relationship whereby they are no longer just identified and recognized as static external environmental supports. The study of resilience has researchers looking beyond just identifying the protective factors. The study of resilience is a quest to dig deeper; it is a quest to understand *how* the protective factors work and contribute to protective processes—what are some of the underlying cognitive, social, emotional, and neurological processes or mechanisms that occur that contribute to resilience? For instance, how do we explain and talk about the protective processes or mechanisms that take place to ultimately achieve the positive outcomes that eventually occur when a student senses that there is a teacher who authentically cares about him or her? What is actually happening inside that student's head, heart, and brain?

Rutter (2006) identifies the study of resilience as a two-step process. He points out that to understand resilience, first one must recognize that individuals interpret experiences differently, and second, one must recognize that resilience implies interactions embedded in a dynamic process. In another two-step definition of resilience, Luthar and Cicchetti (2000) assert that the first step is the empirical identification of the vulnerability and protective factors. The second step, which distinguishes resilience as a unique construct, is the attempt "to understand the mechanisms that might explain the effects of salient vulnerability or protective factors" (p. 859). Thus, saying that there are three protective factors that have been demonstrated to improve young people's educational experience is not enough. In an educational context, student success is not dependent alone upon the static nature of caring relationships, high expectations, and opportunities to participate and contribute. Resilience is a construct that focuses on the internal versus the external; it is not just the fact that these protective factors exist. The study of resilience focuses on how an individual—in the context of this specific book, a student or an education practitioner—interprets, internalizes, and makes meaning out of external factors. In many ways the complexities of the psychological and neurological processes that occur within each individual exposed to the protective factors are what make it necessary to distinguish resilience as a construct and not just a different way of talking about caring relationships, high expectations, and opportunities to participate and contribute. It is not about the "what" of the three protective factors, but rather the "how."

Although there are a variety of definitions used for the construct of resilience, I question many of them with regard to their ability to give enough emphasis to the role that individual perception and cultural and contextual differences have in resilience. Thus I welcome Michael Ungar's (2004) contributions to the definition of resilience alluded to earlier in this chapter in a discussion about "perspective." Ungar argues that most definitions of resilience do not and cannot adequately accommodate the breadth and depth of subjectivity and differentiation that individuals have as they construct meaning out of experiences. Ungar (2004), defining resilience as "the outcome from negotiations between individuals and their environments for the resources to define themselves as healthy amidst conditions collectively viewed as adverse," asserts that appropriate conditions facilitate successful negotiations (p. 342). In an education context at a school or in a classroom, these conditions include caring relationships, high expectations, and opportunities to participate and contribute.

Additional discussions on the topic of resilience and its definition are very insightful because of the interplay between resilience, normative judgment, and subjectivity. These discussions often situate themselves in a political and cultural context asking, Who holds the power and privilege to define resilience? What may be considered a manifestation of resilience to one population may be undesirable to another. This was illustrated in the example I offered earlier of a teen who chooses to be in a gang.

Ultimately, I concur with Ungar as he posits that it would be conceptually wrong for one definition and understanding of resilience to stand alone. Since the construct and study of resilience has emerged in a number of disciplines (e.g. education, psychology, and sociology), I would also suggest that multiple definitions lead to cumulative research, which can enhance the understanding of resilience.

As mentioned earlier, Luthar and colleagues (Luthar et al., 2000a), in a report that supports the contributions that the study of resilience makes to theories of human development, directly respond to a number of issues and criticisms that have been brought up about resilience as a distinct construct. In one argument, they support the study and construct of resilience by highlighting research that demonstrated how two different groups, one with conditions of adversity and one without conditions of adversity, reacted to similar protective factors. The research they highlighted used an example from education. The research "found that the salutary effects of support from school staff were more pronounced among poor youth than others, which suggests that for children facing multiple adversities, the relative dearth of positive experiences outside of school may render those that occur within school even more salient" (p. 553). In another paper, Luthar and colleagues (Luthar et al., 2000b) directly identify the focus on positive indicators among groups typically thought of in terms of their problems as "the strongest single distinguishing feature" of resilience (p. 574). This paper also provides a simple yet significant distinction between resilience research and prevention research. Prevention research focuses on disease avoidance. Resilience research, while also recognizing the absence of disease, disorder, and dysfunction, specifically focuses on wellness and "unexpectedly positive" trajectories of adaptation in the face of adversity (p. 574).

In a section of writing devoted to operationalizing research on resilience, resilience researchers Ann Masten and Jelena Obradovic (2006) note how the study of resilience introduced new models, methods, measures, and strategies of analysis to the research community. It went beyond static features and included elements of time and "the role of combined predictors, mediators, and moderators of good outcomes in the context of risk or adversity" (p. 21). Masten and Obradovic provide a list of adaptive systems that have a role in resilience as a construct in human development. Such adaptive systems include the attachment system incorporating relationships with caregivers, teachers, and friends; stress-response systems comprised of alarm and recovery systems; self-regulation systems, which include emotion regulation, executive functioning, and activation and inhibition of attention or behavior; mastery motivation systems reflecting self-efficacy processes and reward systems related to successful behavior; and school systems, with emphasis on teaching, values, and expectations.

Distinguished sociology researcher Howard B. Kaplan (1999) also took the discussion of resilience, protective factors, and the components that comprise the protective factors into a discussion about methodology, models, and measures. Similar to Masten and Obradovic, Kaplan concerned himself with how protective factors are identified, labeled, and measured: "If protective factors are defined as general constructs or processes consisting of or reflected in several variables, the question arises as to why a general construct rather than the several components should be used" (p. 60). In response to his own question, Kaplan situated the discussion of protective factors in the context of "a process" and suggested specific research methodologies that can further our understanding of the study of resilience and support efforts in developing successful prevention and intervention strategies responsive to such research.

Although a universal definition of resilience, let alone a need for the construct at all, continues to be contested in the research community, a review of the literature clearly identifies much about resilience that the research community does agree upon (e.g., Goldstein & Brooks, 2005). The list from Chapter 1, from the Important Insights from Resilience Research section, provides important findings forwarded from resilience research.

Reflection Section

1. Some of the main concepts, ideas, tools, and/or strategies I learned from this chapter include _____.

2. A personal experience that allows me to relate to the concepts, ideas, tools, and/or strategies presented in the chapter occurred _____.

3. An example of how I have used or will use the concepts, ideas, tools, and/or strategies presented in the chapter in my current practice is _____.

4. In my future practice I would like to build upon the concepts, ideas, tools, and/or strategies presented in the chapter by _____.

5. Ways in which I may need more information, resources, or support to further an understanding or implementation of the concepts, ideas, tools, and/or strategies presented in the chapter are _____.

6. A question I still have about the concepts, ideas, tools, and/or strategies presented in the chapter is _____.

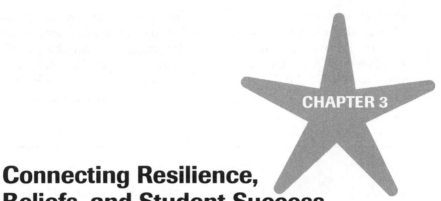

CHAPTER 3

Connecting Resilience, Beliefs, and Student Success

That is still the case in this country for too many students, the soft bigotry of low expectations. If you don't expect them to learn, if you don't expect them to succeed—then it becomes a self-fulfilling prophecy.

—Tavis Smiley

There are few things sadder to a teacher (or parent) than being faced with capable children who, as a result of previous demoralizing experiences, or even self-imposed mind-sets, have come to believe that they cannot learn, when all objective indicators show that they can. Often, much time and patience are required to break the mental habits of perceived incompetence that have come to imprison young minds.

—Frank Pajares, *Schooling in America*

Benard's seminal work on resilience (1991, 2004) posits a theory of resilience applicable to education that identifies the relationship between student needs, elements in an environment, individual strengths, and student success. Simply stated, a student's educational success can be enhanced if a student perceives his or her classroom, school environment, climate, and culture to be one that is caring, communicates high expectations, and provides opportunities for meaningful engagement through student participation and contribution.[1] Findings in resilience and education

---

1. It is important to share that the issue of "safety," which is a major focus in many discussions around school today, as it should be, is inherent in the three protective factors. As an example, safety situates itself in this theory of resilience as an important by-product of caring.

literature and research by a host of researchers and authors (such as Brooks & Goldstein, 2001, 2003, 2004; Brown, D'Emidio-Caston, & Benard, 2001; Henderson & Milstein, 2003; Jessor, 1993; Masten, 1997; Noddings, 2003; Schaps, 2003; and Selig, Arroyo, Lloyd-Zannini, & Jordan, 2006) concur with Benard and demonstrate that educators who employ pedagogical strategies that authentically embrace and develop caring relationships, establish high expectations, and provide opportunities for participation and engagement create a climate, culture, and education environment that positively fosters student resilience, which in turn contributes to quantifiable positive outcomes for students—especially students in high-risk environments. Research that gives students a voice and a say in what the educational system can do to increase and support student success often provides examples where students perceive their classrooms as being void of caring relationships, high expectations, and opportunities to participate and contribute (e.g., Cushman 2003, 2005; Schultz & Cook-Sather, 2001). Researchers Strucker, Moise, Magee, and Kreider (2001) found the following:

> Mentioned more than any other topic . . . was the feeling that teachers really did not care about us as people. We do not deny that some of our teachers showed some interest in us, but our writing showed how much anger and loss we still had toward teachers who rendered us invisible and silent. (p. 155)

This example illustrates the fact that although existing empirical evidence supports the positive benefits of embracing and implementing the resilience theory in education, a disconnect exists between incorporating resilience research into educational policies and practices. Judith Yero (2002), in her book *Teaching in Mind: How Teacher Thinking Shapes Education*, points out that education researcher and Stanford emeritus professor at Stanford University's School of Education Larry Cuban (1995) and psychologist Arthur Combs (1988) attribute this "disconnect" to the fact that many current reforms in education focus solely on "things" that attempt to make education teacher-proof. These "things," such as state and district curricular frameworks and courses of study, are what Cuban refers to as "the official curriculum" (p. 3). Cuban asserts that focusing just on "the official curriculum" ignores other information that is simultaneously being communicated in the classroom by *how* the teacher teaches rather than *what* a teacher teaches. Thus simply changing materials, programs, or specific subject content may alter what is *taught* in a classroom, but may not alter what is *learned*. Once again, an important perspective on education that needs to be communicated and embraced is, It's not *what* you do . . . it's *how* you do it.

UNDERSTANDING THE THEORY OF RESILIENCE

As mentioned earlier, resilience is the dynamic and negotiated process within individuals (internal) and between individuals and their environments (external) for the resources and supports to adapt and define themselves as healthy amid adversity, threat, trauma, and/or everyday stress. Individuals with an interest in increasing positive outcomes and the success of all children and youth can benefit by developing a deeper understanding of the theory of resilience. An understanding of resilience is especially important for individuals who work in education.

Bonnie Benard (2004), in her book *Resiliency: What We Have Learned*, drew upon the work in resilience research and developed a theory of resilience. Figure 3.1 is an illustration of this theory. What follows is an explanation of Benard's theory of resilience as it situates itself in education.

The theory of resilience, Figure 3.1, recognizes that all individuals—children, youth, and adults—have basic human needs, which include but are not limited to the needs for safety, love, belonging, meaning, and accomplishment (Maslow, 1943).

Resilience research consistently finds that three interrelated protective factors (also known as developmental supports and opportunities) together in any single environment—home, school, community, or peer group—play a role in whether these needs are met. The three protective factors are as follows: (1) developing caring relationships, (2) maintaining high expectations, and (3) providing meaningful opportunities for participation and contribution. Once again, when these protective factors are present together in any one environment—home, school, community, or peer group—the climate in that environment becomes one that is optimal for nurturing the resilience of a child, youth, or any individual. Having one protective factor in one environment and another protective factor in a different environment may be helpful, but Benard's theory of resilience stresses that all three protective factors need to be present in just one of the environments to be able to maximize the tapping and fostering of resilience. Furthermore, having all three protective factors in one environment such as in school will compensate for the fact that some of the protective factors are not present in the other environments such as the family, community, or peer group. The protective factors are what provide the developmental supports and opportunities that mitigate and buffer the negative effect that trauma, adversity, and/or stress may have on an individual. As the illustration of the theory indicates, the protective factors contribute to the healthy and successful development and emergence of the individual's personal developmental competencies and strengths (see Appendix A). These include strengths such as social competence (social skills involving relationships,

Figure 3.1. Theory of resilience

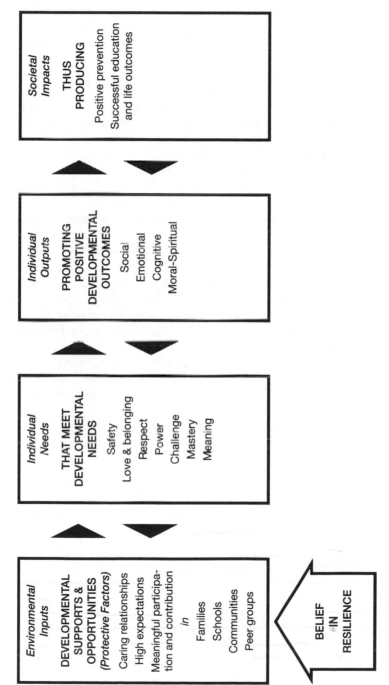

Environmental Inputs	Individual Needs	Individual Outputs	Societal Impacts
DEVELOPMENTAL SUPPORTS & OPPORTUNITIES *(Protective Factors)*	**THAT MEET DEVELOPMENTAL NEEDS**	**PROMOTING POSITIVE DEVELOPMENTAL OUTCOMES**	**THUS PRODUCING**
Caring relationships	Safety	Social	Positive prevention
High expectations	Love & belonging	Emotional	Successful education
Meaningful participation and contribution	Respect	Cognitive	and life outcomes
in	Power	Moral-Spiritual	
Families	Challenge		
Schools	Mastery		
Communities	Meaning		
Peer groups			

BELIEF IN RESILIENCE

Source: Benard, 2004.

31

responsiveness, flexibility, empathy, caring, communication, compassion, altruism, and forgiveness); the ability to problem-solve (cognitive skills such as planning, flexibility, critical thinking, insight, and resourcefulness); autonomy (emotional skills fostering one's sense of self, including positive identity, internal locus of control, self-efficacy, initiative, self-awareness, and adaptive distancing); and sense of purpose and future (goal direction and moral and spiritual aspects, including sense of meaning, optimism, hope, imagination, creativity, motivation, educational aspirations, persistence, spiritual connectedness, and faith).

It is then that individuals' strengths and outcomes contribute to a reduction in their health risks and/or unhealthy behavior and a continued increase in their healthy development, positive well-being, educational success, and life success. In addition to the positive outcomes that individuals experience, it is important to note that individual strengths and positive development outcomes also contribute collectively to an increase in successful community and societal outcomes. A good example of this would be if students, teachers, staff, and parents in a school are supported in their own resilience. Then the school itself, as a community, has the capacity to manifest its resilience in a time of difficulty or crisis. This has been evident in trying times such as the mass shootings in Newtown, Connecticut, and Littleton, Colorado, and with natural disasters as experienced in Hurricane Katrina in New Orleans and Hurricane Sandy in the Northeast.

As mentioned earlier and as depicted by the large arrow at the bottom of Figure 3.1, the process of fostering resilience and being able to consistently provide the protective factors (caring relationships, high expectations, opportunities to participate and contribute) in any environment (home, school, community, or peer group), for ourselves or others, begins by believing that all individuals have the capacity for resilience.

WHAT ARE BELIEFS?

Like resilience, the concept of "beliefs" lends itself to a multitude of definitions. And just like resilience, there are some constants. Inherent in most definitions of beliefs is the understanding and acknowledgment that beliefs are socially constructed and often personal assumptions, judgments, generalizations, opinions, inferences, conceptions, conclusions, evaluations, and the like that we make about ourselves and the people, places, and things around us. Although the definition of beliefs may differ among researchers, one commonality that often does emerge is the claim that beliefs are constructed and inferred. Frank Pajares (1992), an education psychologist whose research and interests included beliefs, self-efficacy, and student motivation, provides one of the more pithy and direct definitions of beliefs by contrasting it to knowledge: "Belief is based on evaluation and judgment; knowledge is based on objective fact" (p. 313).

Beliefs are socially constructed. Judith Yero (2002), in her book *Teaching in Mind: How Teacher Thinking Shapes Education*, refers to beliefs "as judgments and evaluations that we make about ourselves, about others, and about the world around us. Beliefs are *generalizations* about things such as causality or the meaning of specific *actions*" (p. 21). This understanding is vitally important to educators because teacher differences in attitudes and beliefs can negatively or positively affect student success. Teacher attitudes and beliefs about students can differ based upon factors such as a student's race, ethnicity, social class, disability, and gender.

WHAT DO WE MEAN WHEN WE TALK ABOUT STUDENT SUCCESS?

A great deal of dialogue has centered on operationally defining "student success." An unfortunate mindset of many stakeholders in education is to define student success strictly by the quantitative data that are directly reported from the results of standardized testing instruments. The federal policy initiative No Child Left Behind Act of 2001 (No Child Left Behind [NCLB], 2002) has been recognized as a catalyst in supporting this mindset.

Fortunately, stakeholders in education are finding research that is strengthening and supporting the argument that to determine the success or failure of students' success solely based on how they perform on standardized tests may, in fact, *not* be the best way to measure success (e.g., Halpern, 2004; New York Times, 2012; Noddings, 2003; Schaps, 2000). In fact, it could be detrimental—not only to the education system but also, and more importantly, to the students themselves (Nichols & Berliner, 2007; Noddings, 2003; Olson, 2009).

Using a conceptual framework of resilience includes having a more inclusive definition of student success other than one based upon grades and standardized test scores. Student success includes mastering skills, gaining knowledge, and having qualities that prepare students as productive and contributing members in our global and ever-changing world. Successful students have developed a passion for learning that serves them throughout adulthood as creative, innovative, and persistent problem-solvers and thinkers. Simply stated, student success is achieved by those who progress on a positive trajectory that leads them to become healthy, independent, civil, respectful, empathetic, caring, contributing members of society—individuals who are whole—academically, socially, physically, emotionally, and spiritually.

HOW DO WE GET FROM TEACHER BELIEFS IN
STUDENT RESILIENCE TO STUDENT SUCCESS?

A number of processes occur that can explain how we get from teacher beliefs in student resilience to student success. Like many aspects of human behavior, a number of aspects of the construct of resilience cannot be explained within the context of one discipline. How teachers' positive beliefs translate into providing their students with the protective factors associated with fostering resilience can best be answered by highlighting some of the research that helps explain the relationship between the individuals in the situation and the respective neurological, biological, and psychological experiences that may be occurring within them. Approaching this question in this way is within the context of what resilience researchers Ann Masten and Jelena Obradovic (2006) recognize as the fourth wave of resilience research.

> The first three waves of research on resilience in development, largely behavioral in focus, contributed a compelling set of concepts and methods, a surprisingly consistent body of findings, provocative issues and controversies, and clues to promising areas for the next wave of resilience research linking biology and neuroscience to behavioral adaptation in development. Their findings implicate fundamental adaptive systems, which in turn suggest hot spots for the rising fourth wave of integrative research on resilience in children, focused on processes studied at multiple levels of analysis and across species. (p. 13)

Mark Greenberg (2006), director of the Prevention Research Center for the Promotion of Human Development at Pennsylvania State University, states, "Such work . . . should take us past the 'black box' outcome to more fully understand the cognitive and neural mediators and moderators of change" (p. 147).

Luthar, Sawyer, and Brown (2006) identify "the need to unpack underlying processes" (p. 106) as one of the critical conceptual issues in resilience research. It is in this spirit that I will begin with a brief discussion from a neurological perspective on beliefs.

As stated earlier, beliefs are socially constructed and often personal assumptions, judgments, generalizations, opinions, inferences, conceptions, conclusions, evaluations, and the like that we make about ourselves and the people, places, and things around us. Much of belief research focuses on understanding how beliefs affect and influence an individual's behavior (e.g., Behar, Pajares, & George, 1996; Guskey, 1986; Hollingsworth, 1989; Munby, 1982). Research informs us that differences in attitudes, attributions, and beliefs affect and influence not only educators, but also social workers, medical practitioners, and police officers (Norgaard, 2005). The attitudes, attributions, and beliefs of these practitioners can negatively or positively affect their decisions for interventions and practices that ultimately affect their clients' and students' outcomes.

Similar to belief researchers, researchers studying attribution theory and mindsets (Hong, Dweck, Chiu, Lin, & Wan, 1999; Weiner, 1990) focus on understanding how one's cognitive schema affects and influences practice. Attribution theorists suggest that individuals striving to make sense of the world make inferences based upon their own internal (personal) and external (situational) factors. J. Michael Norgaard (2005) cautions:

> The problem that can arise from the use of these preconceived attributions is that they may leave an individual less open to change or consideration of other perspectives. Once this occurs, a risk of becoming locked into outdated belief systems that become self-perpetuating through their repeated application to events in the environment develops. (p. 2)

Current research highlights the plasticity of the brain and often compares it to a muscle, indicating that the more it is used, the stronger it becomes (Feuerstein, Feuerstein, & Falik, 2010; La Cerra & Bingham, 2002; Perry, 2002; Siegel, 2010). Neurologists have explored what happens neurologically when individuals become locked in belief systems. It affects their neural circuitry and their responses to certain situations and stimuli. Locked patterns of beliefs can be positive and/or negative. Optimism and hope and the belief that all students have the capacity for resilience are examples of positive beliefs that can be learned. Researchers studying the plasticity of the brain found that positive or negative repeated patterns of thought and/or exposure to positive or negative experiences—either as a onetime incident such as a cataclysmic event or as a repeated experience such as physical or mental abuse—all contribute to neurological changes and developments in the brain. In using this book as a tool in a preservice program for new educators and administrators or in a professional development experience for current and veteran educators, I hope to influence a shift in practitioners' thinking, which also may influence a neurological shift. I hope to have teachers and administrators understand the fundamentals of resilience and recognize that resilience does not reside as a trait in a person or as a single attribute in an environment, but rather as a neurological as well as psychological process and interaction between an individual and the environment. In addition, I hope to convey to all adults in the education system a general understanding and awareness of how their interactions with students affect how those students' brains may receive and interpret information and how such neurological processes can affect students psychologically, biologically, physically, and academically.

I agree that it is important for educators to understand the plasticity in the neural circuitry of resilience and emotion and its implications for how social experiences have an effect on being able to cultivate positive affect and resilience in humans through social experiences (Committee on Integrating the Science of Early Childhood Development, 2000). In fact, I feel that it would not be appropriate to discuss the process of resilience *without* acknowledging the fact that it is more than just a psychological process. Yet I also am concerned that the excitement of what we are learning in neuroscience can at times pull resources away from what we already know works and can implement. Thus I will now touch upon some of the psychological processes that, when understood, help to "unpack" the "black box" of resilience.

As I suggested earlier, part of the reason why it is difficult to talk about the psychological processes that occur with beliefs and resilience is because of the complexities and difficulties inherent in the constructs. One difficulty relates to the terminology and semantics. Frank Pajares (1992) conveys this by saying that beliefs "travel in disguise and often under alias" (p. 309). Researchers Jean Clandinin and Michael Connelly (1987) talk about the "bewildering array of terms" that are used when discussing the concept of beliefs (p. 487). Some of these aliases and terms include the following: *opinions, conclusions, dispositions, conceptions, judgments, ideology, conceptual systems, implicit theories, explicit theories,* and *values.*

Another difficulty that adds to the complexity of belief research is the fact that it can be discussed within the context of a number of different dynamic psychological processes, with explanations from a variety of approaches in psychology. Once again Frank Pajares (1992) articulates this complexity:

> Self-efficacy . . . is a cornerstone of social cognitive theory. Self-concept and self-esteem are the essence of phenomenological and humanistic theories. Studies on attribution beliefs and locus of control are also prominent in investigations of student thought processes, and interest in epistemological beliefs is growing. Subject specific beliefs, such as beliefs about reading, mathematics, or the nature of science, are key to researchers' attempting to understand the intricacies of how children learn. The information processing approach focuses on the characteristics of learners, including not only self-beliefs, such as self-concept and self-efficacy, but also beliefs about the nature of intelligence, of knowledge, and of motivations. (p. 308)

Although there are a number of explanations in psychology to discuss this phenomenon, it would be close to impossible for research to offer one comprehensive psychological explanation regarding what the underlying processes are that contribute to resilience. This is because of the different ways each individual responds and interacts to factors in the environment. As discussed in Chapter 2, the issues of locus of control, time, perspective, culture, context, power, privilege, and subjectivity complicate the ability to have one explanation as to what underlying processes occur to promote or manifest resilience. Even though it is impossible to offer a comprehensive and single psychological explanation, what follows is an attempt to highlight some of the psychological processes, out of many, that are embedded in the study of resilience in education when discussing the relationship between beliefs about student resilience and student success.

We can discuss beliefs, attitudes, and dispositions within the context of the following three psychological components: cognitive, affective, and behavioral. In a classroom context, the cognitive focuses on what a teacher believes about a student. The affective component relates to a teacher's feelings about a student. The behavioral component is about the behavior that a teacher displays when interacting with a student.

Rutgers psychology professor Lee Jussim (1986), in his discussion on self-fulfilling prophecies in the classroom, offers a model and a comprehensive discussion of the psychological and sociological processes that explain how "a teacher's expectations about a student's future achievement evoke from the student performance levels consistent with the teacher's expectations" (p. 429). His model is composed of three broad stages: teacher expectations, differential treatment, and students' reactions. Jussim provides an in-depth discussion of his model and indicates that it begins with a teacher's initial expectations and beliefs, which can often be erroneous and ultimately detrimental to a student's future success in school.

Beliefs about students and education develop in a number of ways. Teachers and adults can often develop beliefs and base future expectations on information gathered without even interacting with a student, such as identifying that student with a sibling or family, or talking to another teacher who may have had a certain type of interaction with that student. Teachers and adults in a school can also develop beliefs based upon early and limited assessments, evaluations, and academic tests. Some beliefs come from our own personal experiences. In fact, many teachers, administrators, and policymakers in education revert to their own memories and the personal school experiences they had in their youth as a prominent source of what they believe about education today—regardless of how many years have transpired or how much science has advanced since they were students. Attribution theorists suggest that individuals striving to make sense of the world make inferences based upon their own internal (personal) and external (situational) factors. While some beliefs are attributed to memories, still other beliefs are "taken for granted" or developed by chance.

The preservice or professional development experience on resilience that I propose in this book begins by relating information about the concept of resilience. At this level, participants engage in learning about the concept of resilience and the relationship that beliefs have with resilience—resilience starts with what one believes. One of these beliefs is that all students have the capacity for resilience.[2] As that information is relayed, the teacher on a very basic level will either accept or reject the belief based upon his/her current beliefs that are rooted in experiences and other factors, as mentioned earlier. If the belief is congruent with what is already embraced by the practitioner, then the message should serve as a confirmation of his or her original belief. If the message is not congruent with the practitioner's current beliefs about students, then the practitioner may reject what is being heard. Throughout my personal involvement and work in policy, education, and research, I have experienced the constructive nature of cognitive conflict and dissonance and the importance of providing preservice and veteran teachers with safe environments so that they can engage in reflective practices that encourage them to explore their current beliefs, recognize their resistance to change, and challenge their beliefs. Beliefs to be explored might include beliefs about teaching, learning, and diversity—beliefs that have definite implications for how teachers teach and how students learn. These implications can be discussed within the context of psychology.

Yero (2002) identifies three psychological factors that are significant to teacher effectiveness and student success. They are self-efficacy, locus of control, and pupil-control ideology. Yero quotes from the study of Agne, Greenwood, and Miller (1994) that "teachers with a high sense of efficacy were more likely than their low-efficacy counterparts to define low achieving students as reachable, teachable and worthy of teacher attention and effort" (p. 142). Teachers with an internal locus of control, as opposed to an external locus of control, believe that their actions are meaningful and responsible for producing outcomes. Yero talks about pupil-control ideology and shares that control beliefs range from *custodial* to *humanistic*. She defines custodial beliefs as those that are highly controlling, employ punishment, have impersonal relationships with students, possess attitudes of mistrust, and focus on the maintenance of order. Humanistic beliefs, on the other hand, encourage participation and communication; develop close and caring relationships with students; and demonstrate mutual respect, flexibility of rules, and positive attitudes. Teachers who embrace and demonstrate humanistic beliefs also foster students' independence, self-determination, and self-discipline. Teachers who embrace the belief that all students have

---

2. This is not to diminish the fact that there may be neurological and/or genetic conditions that compromise the development of resilience in some individuals (Rutter, 2006)

the capacity for resilience are teachers who embrace humanistic beliefs. Having high self-efficacy, internal locus of control, and humanistic beliefs can affect a teacher's motivation to engage students. This can, in turn, have a profound positive effect upon student motivation and learning, especially for students from high-risk environments.

Studies in fields such as cognitive, behavior, social, and positive psychology that explore phenomena and concepts such as self-fulfilling prophecy, motivation, optimism, and hope have shown that teachers whose practices reflect their belief that all students have the capacity for resilience communicate and use language that conveys psychological messages to students that get internalized and processed in manners that positively affect their success in school.

In another discussion about psychological processes, Greenberg (2006) talks about something else that can manifest in an educational environment—the psychological cognitive and emotion-regulation skills identified with the psychological processes attributed to stress:

> Central components of the stress response include the initial appraisal of the event and its emotional meaning, the ability to sufficiently regulate one's emotions and arousal to initiate problem solving and gather more information, the fuller cognitive-affective interpretation of the event, and one's behavioral response. (p. 141) *emotional regulation*

As mentioned in the Preface, schools are often seen by many as a place that perpetuates stress. In thinking about this stress response, it is important to consider how a classroom environment that is warm, caring, and trusting could possibly diminish or mitigate a debilitating stress response from a student. Although teachers may not have a deep understanding of the psychological processes that are embedded in resilience, teachers who intuitively provide the three protective factors in their classroom generate positive student outcomes. As the students continue on a positive trajectory of school success, not only academically but also socially and emotionally, the teachers' intuitive beliefs about how to motivate and support students are supported. Thus teachers become equipped with a craft knowledge that encourages them to continue what they are doing in their practice.

As I reflect upon my work, I find myself agreeing with Luthar, Sawyer, and Brown (2006), who while supporting the genetic and neurological components of resilience and the need to continue work in this area, are pragmatic with respect to the limited funds and resources devoted to resilience research: "The reality is that as we devote more to studying biology and genes, we have that much less toward developing creative interventions to alter factors that we already *know very well* can make an enormous difference" (p. 110). Thus I contend that preservice and professional development experiences that spend some time unpacking and disseminating information to educators about the psychological and neurological relationships that beliefs have with resilience can support the goal of transferring resilience research into practice with the intent of supporting the health, success, and well-being of *everyone* psychologically, neurologically, and in all the other ways that nurture and contribute to positive development and learning.

Reflection Section

1. Some of the main concepts, ideas, tools, and/or strategies I learned from this chapter include _____.

2. A personal experience that allows me to relate to the concepts, ideas, tools, and/or strategies presented in the chapter occurred _____.

3. An example of how I have used or will use the concepts, ideas, tools, and/or strategies presented in the chapter in my current practice is _____.

4. In my future practice I would like to build upon the concepts, ideas, tools, and/or strategies presented in the chapter by _____.

5. Ways in which I may need more information, resources, or support to further an understanding or implementation of the concepts, ideas, tools, and/or strategies presented in the chapter are _____.

6. A question I still have about the concepts, ideas, tools, and/or strategies presented in the chapter is _____.

More on Beliefs

Whether you think you can or whether you think you can't, you're right.
—Henry Ford

Men often become what they believe themselves to be. If I believe I cannot do something, it makes me incapable of doing it. But when I believe I can, then I acquire the ability to do it even if I didn't have it in the beginning.
—Mohandas Gandhi

In order to believe in our students, we first have to see our students—literally. One of the most dramatic, enlightening, and even heartbreaking activities that I did around the issue of resilience and beliefs occurred when I discussed those two concepts within the context of developing authentic and caring relationships with students.

I was doing a professional development day for the staff who worked with students in grades 6 through 8 at a middle school. Prior to the day of the professional development, I requested that the principal prepare a roster of the whole student body. The roster was prepared in alphabetical order. It was then divided into segments and placed on the walls around the room.

At the beginning of the professional development, I shared a quote from the research of Emmy Werner and Ruth Smith (1989):

> Among the most frequently encountered positive role models in the lives of the children . . . outside of the family circle, was a favorite teacher. For the resilient youngster a special teacher was not just an instructor for academic skills, but also a confidante and positive model for personal identification. (p. 162)

I then gave everyone a pack of sticky dots. I told the staff that what I wanted them to do was sometime during the course of the day, get up and go to the charts and put a dot of theirs next to any student with whom they feel they have a relationship. I defined *relationship* as the ability to know the student's name and ask that student a question or start a conversation with that student about something meaningful in his or her life that did not have anything do with school, such as, "Allen, how was your basketball game last night?" or "Amy, how was your weekend hike in the park?" or "Lynn, how was your visit this weekend with your relatives?"

At the end of the day, after everyone had the chance to go to the charts and place their sticky dots, I directed everyone's attention to the charts. An incredibly dramatic visual appeared. As you can imagine, there were some students whom everyone seemed to know and have a relationship with—these were students with a slew of stickers after their names. But the heartbreaking part was the sight of a number of students who had no dots after their names—and it included students who had been at the school for all 3 years! This visual was dramatic, enlightening, and created quite a shock to the staff as they continued to ask themselves, "How is it that a student could be in our school for 3 years and not have a relationship with one adult in the school?" Yes, it was shocking—not to mention depressing. Yet within minutes the depressing energy that emanated from such shock was reframed and made productive. The staff saw an incredible opportunity—the opportunity to purposefully do something about that. And this is what the staff decided to do . . .

After the professional development, the principal took the list from the wall. Any students with four dots or fewer by their names had their names transferred to a different roster. The principal then took the names and divided them into equal groups according to the ratio of student names to staff. Each staff person was given the same number of names and the same directive: It was their opportunity to begin to create and foster an authentic and caring relationship with each student on their list. Time was provided at subsequent staff meetings for the staff to talk about how they were doing in creating these relationships and what tips they might share with each other in navigating the process. For example, how did they start conversations? What worked? What didn't work? Time was also provided at staff meetings to continue "processing the process" as well as reaffirming the positive value of creating such relationships.

I continue to think about how that simple exercise of putting dots next to names has the potential to change the lives of some students who might otherwise go through school as "ghost students." Yes, resilience begins with beliefs, yet how can we begin to believe in our students if we don't even see them?

WHY ARE BELIEFS SO IMPORTANT?

Teacher beliefs influence teacher practices (e.g., Ferguson, 2003; Tatto, 1996). Research has shown that teachers' beliefs and perceptions about education, teaching, learning, and student achievement affect not only their pedagogical practices but also student efficacy and success (e.g., Akey, 2006; Bamburg, 1994; Obiakor, 2000; Ryan & Patrick, 2001). This is very powerful, especially since a teacher's beliefs and perceptions about a particular student's achievement can be developed without regard to prior knowledge about, or experience with, that particular student's ability. Evidence supports the idea that students' perceptions and beliefs about their own abilities and capacity for learning can positively or negatively be affected by a teacher's perceptions and beliefs (Andrews, Soder, & Jacoby, 1986; Brophy & Everston, 1981; Brophy & Good, 1970; Jussim, 1986; McDonald & Elias, 1976; Rutter, 1979; Ryan & Patrick, 2001). Studies exploring the relationship between teachers' beliefs and student success have been documented. Bamburg (1994) investigated the relationship between teachers' expectations of students and student learning. Jussim (1986) studied the social and psychological processes of the self-fulfilling prophecy and the role that teacher expectations have in affecting student outcomes. Hughes (1995) characterized effective schools as ones where teachers maintain strong beliefs that children can achieve. With reference to specific beliefs, Love (2003) investigated the relationship between teachers' culturally relevant beliefs and student achievement for African American students in urban schools. Schirmer and colleagues (Schirmer, Casbon, & Twiss, 1997) looked at how some teachers' beliefs about students with learning disabilities may have thwarted student success because the deep-rooted beliefs impaired the teachers' ability to approach teaching and learning for students with disabilities in new ways.

In related studies, self-efficacy and collective efficacy beliefs and perceptions in academic settings have been a topic of considerable investigation (e.g., Bandura, 1993; Goddard, 2003; Pajares, 1996; Purkey, 1979; Schunk, 1982). *Collective efficacy* describes the cumulative effect of what happens when a collective system such as a school, including administration, teachers, and students, maintains high expectations of levels of attainment for a particular system. The effect of an individual teacher's beliefs and the effect of multiple teachers' beliefs as part of collective efficacy have been recognized in research to mitigate and mediate negative student outcomes that are often attributed to students' socioeconomic status and prior academic achievement.

WHAT DOES THE RESEARCH SAY ABOUT AFFECTING BELIEFS?

The ability to influence beliefs is a difficult and daunting task, yet because teachers' belief systems can influence and orient their practice, the development of high-quality teachers often resides in the ability to challenge their beliefs.

Education research on teacher beliefs focuses on understanding how teacher beliefs affect and influence teacher practices and student outcomes. Pohan and Aguilar (2001) identify research indicating that teacher differences in attitudes and beliefs can negatively or positively affect student success. Teacher attitudes and beliefs about students can differ based upon factors such as a student's race, ethnicity, social class, learning differences, and gender. A teacher's attitudes and beliefs—whether consciously or subconsciously—about a student's resilience will also negatively or positively influence a teacher's behavior, actions, and practices, and subsequently, a student's success.

Because the resilience process begins with what one believes, the process of promoting resilience begins by believing that all individuals have the capacity for resilience. Once again, the list in Chapter 1, under the heading Important Insights from Resilience Research, provides examples of positive beliefs about individuals that should be embraced.

When people who work with children and youth, especially children and youth exposed to adversity or stress, authentically and sincerely believe in the resilience of the children, youth, and families they work with, they naturally convey the attributes of a caring relationship, especially empathic listening and patience. They also communicate high-expectation messages to the children, youth, and families with whom they work—messages that as the children, youth, and families continue to negotiate and gain exposure to resources within themselves and externally in their environments, they will become more empowered with everything they need to succeed and will embrace the belief that their strengths will help them address challenges. Similarly, a resilient belief system, one that sees children, youth, and families as resources, will engage them as active participants in working through challenging situations as they look for meaningful opportunities that promote their ability to contribute and participate in activities that will promote healthy outcomes.

Mr. H, a teacher I worked with in a continuation high school in Oakland, California, provides a wonderful example of how he conveys his belief in the resilience of his students. He talks about "the genius" that resides inside all his students:

> In terms of students in my particular case, it's the one thing that stuck with me all year and I use it almost every day . . . this concept of "genius" . . . at this point it is just part of my activity and when students are interacting with me, for instance today—there's this new student [names student], and we're doing a mock test and there was something that we covered a couple of days ago, and he says, "Well I don't know but I think it's this." And I said, "Yes! You see you are a genius—you had the thought in mind." And I've been talking about

and they get a little thrill—at least I get a thrill, I'm hoping that they get a thrill too—I'm pointing out that, "look, this is what you have—you have this innate ability" and in my situation that has been my focus . . . resilience has become "genius" and I keep working on the "genius." (Truebridge, 2010, p. 95)

Reflection Section

1. Some of the main concepts, ideas, tools, and/or strategies I learned from this chapter include _____.

2. A personal experience that allows me to relate to the concepts, ideas, tools, and/or strategies presented in the chapter occurred _____.

3. An example of how I have used or will use the concepts, ideas, tools, and/or strategies presented in the chapter in my current practice is _____.

4. In my future practice I would like to build upon the concepts, ideas, tools, and/or strategies presented in the chapter by _____.

5. Ways in which I may need more information, resources, or support to further an understanding or implementation of the concepts, ideas, tools, and/or strategies presented in the chapter are _____.

6. A question I still have about the concepts, ideas, tools, and/or strategies presented in the chapter is _____.

CHAPTER 5

Influencing Beliefs, Fostering Resilience, and Promoting Student Success: It's a Process, Not a Program

We discovered that education is not something which the teacher does, but that it is a natural process which develops spontaneously in the human being.

—Maria Montessori

Facilitating resilience is more a matter of orientation than explicit intervention . . . it insists that you hold a broad view of growth and change, realizing that there are always untapped degrees of freedom for the motivated to mobilize.

—Gina O'Connell Higgins, *Resilient Adults*

Creating an environment that fosters resilience in students does not necessitate an exorbitant amount of money or time. There is no dearth of research or information on how a positive classroom school climate and culture lead to positive educational and life success. In fact, creating a positive classroom and school climate and culture has become a major focus of today's school reform and transformation efforts. That's great news! The unfortunate news is that many schools and policymakers are still looking for a "quick fix" in an effort to create a positive school climate and culture and this has led to a number of new curricula and programs that are being sold to schools under the guise of being able to quickly transform a school's culture and

▷ shocking (insert eye roll here)

climate. Unfortunately, transforming a school's culture and climate is more than buying a new curriculum or new program. Programs and curricula still have to be implemented. And unfortunately, efforts that focus on prescribed curricula, programs, and materials ignore the role of other information that simultaneously gets communicated in the classroom through implementation—in other words, by *how* the teacher teaches rather than *what* a teacher teaches.

Education is about both teaching and learning, and although subject content can improve what is being taught in a classroom, it still can ignore what is actually learned. Students absorb more than the objective and content information that needs to be conveyed through a specific curriculum or program. Students learn about the affective nature of interactions and what occurs "in the spaces" of a lesson and a day. What tone of voice is being used? What words are being used? What facial expressions are used? How does the teacher deal with interruptions and discord? How are transitions handled? Creating a climate and culture that promotes, supports, and sustains resilience is accomplished by embracing the understanding that it is not *what* you do, but rather *how* you do what you do. How you teach what you teach. How you interact in your relationships. How you physically create and use space. It is about what we model every day, every minute, and with every interaction. Those are the true elements that create the climate and culture in our classrooms and our schools. By now it should be clear that resilience is a process, not a program.

THE CONCEPTUAL FRAMEWORK THAT GUIDES THE PROCESS

As I mentioned in the Introduction, the important question that drove my research for my dissertation was, How do educators respond to a professional development program on the concept of resilience? I framed it this way, specifically without the mention of beliefs, because I wanted my research question to explore whether the concepts of beliefs and practices emerged from the participants themselves as they engaged in the professional development process. And sure enough they did. That led me to develop a conceptual framework that I have since found to hold constant as I continue to facilitate professional development experiences for teachers and administrators of schools at various grade levels within rural, suburban, and urban settings.

Figure 5.1 provides a comprehensive conceptual framework illustrating a process of how an education preservice and professional development experience can influence teacher beliefs and affect student outcomes.

Figure 5.1. The framework and context for understanding the process of how a preservice and professional development experience can influence teacher beliefs and affect student outcomes

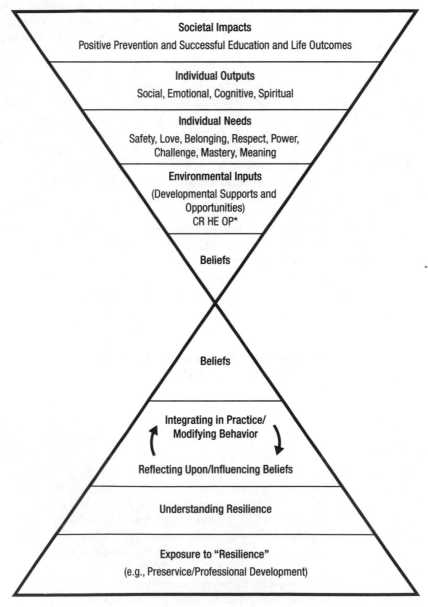

*CR = caring relationships; HE = high expectations; OP = opportunites to participate.

Note: The top inverted triangle is from Benard & Marshall, 1997.

The hourglass figure is comprised of two triangles. The conceptual framework begins at the bottom triangle with exposure to resilience and progresses up to societal impact. The top triangle is adapted from Bonnie Benard and Kathy Marshall's (1997) work and reflects the theory of resilience that is explained in Chapter 3 and Figure 3.1. (Instead of being depicted horizontally as it was in Chapter 3, here it is depicted in a triangle with the same understanding that the process is dynamic and the divisions between the sections are permeable and go in both directions, up and down—as they went from both left to right and vice versa when the theory was depicted horizontally.) The bottom triangle was developed as a result of my research and work in the area of resilience and begins where the previous resilience research left off with recognizing that resilience begins with beliefs.

The following list (similar to the one found in Chapter 1 under Important Insights from Resilience Research) provides examples of positive beliefs about student resilience that educators should authentically embrace:

- Resilience is a process, not a trait.
- All people have the capacity for resilience.
- Most individuals do make it despite exposure to severe risk.
- Coming from a risk environment does not
  determine individual outcomes.
- Bad behavior does not equate with being a bad person.
- One person can make a difference in the life of another person.
- Challenging life experiences and events can be
  opportunities for growth, development, and change.
- Many personal strengths are associated with resilience.
- Three major environmental protective factors can be identified
  that mitigate adversities and nourish personal strengths:
  1. Caring relationships
  2. High expectations
  3. Opportunities to participate and contribute
- As a practitioner, it is how you do what you do that counts.
- To help others you need to help yourself;
  resilience is a parallel process.
- Resilience begins with beliefs.

Exposure to the Concept of Resilience

Affecting practitioners' and administrators' belief systems about student resilience through well-designed and supported preservice or professional development experiences are two concrete ways to transfer resilience research into practice. This begins by recognizing teachers as scholars and providing them with enough research that values them, empowers them, and enables them to understand the concept of resilience as they progress toward authentically embracing (or reconfirming) the belief that all students have the capacity for resilience. All or parts of Chapters 1–4, which provide an educational context, a historical context, and a theoretical understanding of resilience, can be used for this purpose. As I have said before, well-designed and well-implemented teacher preservice and professional development experiences can and should provide participants with a working understanding and awareness of resilience in themselves and in the students with whom they work.

Understanding Resilience

Although practitioners and administrators can develop an understanding of resilience, understanding a concept does not always mean that it will be transferred seamlessly into practice, nor does it mean that the concept automatically influences one's belief system. I am cognizant that simply dispensing information on resilience and belief research through a preservice or professional development experience is not sufficient. Some people, even when they hold a belief that contradicts what they have been taught about best practices in preservice education or professional development, continue to engage in practices that are more aligned to their long-held original beliefs. Disseminating information about the relationship between resilience and beliefs may not be enough for educators to change their current practice.

Influencing Beliefs and Integrating Resilience into Practice

The ability to influence beliefs is a difficult and daunting task, yet because teachers' belief systems can influence and orient their practice, the development of high-quality teachers often resides in the ability to challenge their beliefs. Although the definition of beliefs may differ semantically across the disciplines, one commonality that often emerges is the claim that beliefs are constructed and inferred, while knowledge is based on fact (e.g., Nespor, 1987). Research supports the claim that the longer one has held on to a belief, the harder it is to change that belief. Some of these beliefs about students lead to teacher practices founded on beliefs that may not be warranted and may not foster optimal student outcomes (Plata & Masten, 1998).

It is important to note how the word *influence* situates itself in this discussion. *Merriam-Webster's Online Dictionary* (2009) defines the word *influence* as "the act or power of producing an effect without apparent exertion of force or direct exercise of command" and "the power or capacity of causing an effect in indirect or intangible ways." It is important to recognize that within the context of this definition, *influence* is not synonymous with *change*. Thus the nuances, distinctions, and semantics regarding "influencing beliefs about student resilience" include the act of making currently held beliefs about student resilience more salient. Furthermore, and although extreme, change of beliefs can come about through violence and force, whereas the word *influence* implies independent empowerment and choice.

The research I conducted for my dissertation in 2010 found that there are practitioners who come to their practice already having positive beliefs about student resilience. In fact, that is what draws certain individuals into education. Yet because of circumstances, such beliefs may wane. In situations such as these, the act of influencing practitioners' beliefs, especially through preservice or professional development experiences, is directed more at having practitioners engage in opportunities and/or activities that allow them to influence their beliefs by "reflecting" upon their originally held positive beliefs, thus providing validation and continued purpose to their lives and to the work and service that they continue to pursue.

Although beliefs that transfer into practices can be influenced through well-designed preservice and professional development experiences, education researchers Thomas Guskey (1986) and Michael Fullan (2008) both talk about how the directionality of beliefs and practices can work the other way—there are times (refer to the example of the math teacher provided in the Introduction) when a teacher's practices can influence his/her beliefs. This is captured in the hourglass figure of the conceptual framework and reflected by the arrows that point in both directions.

This leads to the peak of the bottom triangle. The belief that is represented at the peak of the bottom triangle is the same belief that is represented by the bottom section of the top triangle: the belief that all students have the capacity for resilience. Practitioners who have this belief are equipped with some of the most important tools of education that will successfully support them as they support others—empathy, compassion, hope, optimism, self-efficacy, and understanding that they can make a difference.

As illustrated in Figure 5.1, the bottom triangle provides a process that "fits under" the conceptual framework developed by Benard and Marshall. When the triangles are put together as in Figure 5.1, they provide a comprehensive conceptual framework indicating a process for supporting educators as they understand and transfer resilience and belief research into educational practice.

WHAT MIGHT THIS PROCESS LOOK LIKE FOR PRESERVICE AND PROFESSIONAL DEVELOPMENT?

Thomas Guskey (1986) defines professional development as "a systematic attempt to bring about change—change in the classroom practices of teachers, change in their beliefs and attitudes, and change in the learning outcomes of students" (p. 5). Thoughtful and deliberate staff development and preservice education that incorporate inquiry, narratives, storytelling, and reflective practices to enhance self-awareness provide two venues where teacher beliefs about student resilience, especially as such beliefs relate to students from high-risk environments, may be challenged, modified, and translated into pedagogical practices that enhance high-quality teaching and student success.

MORE THAN JUST DISPENSING INFORMATION

I am cognizant that in keeping with this research, simply dispensing information on resilience research through an education preservice or professional development experience is not sufficient. In an effort to maximize and meet outcome measures, such a professional development and/or preservice experience needs to "walk the talk" and be systematic and aware not just about *what* is taught, but more important, *how* it is taught. Research supports that providing practitioners with reflective practices and opportunities, both of which enhance self-awareness and challenge beliefs about student resilience, should be incorporated into education preservice and professional development experiences (Schon, 1991).

As I have mentioned, providing preservice and professional development does not always easily or quickly transfer into practice. However, well-designed, well-implemented, and supported preservice and professional development opportunities enhance the prospects that high-quality research about "best practices" will actually transfer into a practitioner's practice and be sustained. Preservice and/or professional development experiences provide opportunities to support practitioners in their exploration and their capacity to be their own agents of change as a catalyst to activate, enhance, and support their students' belief in the powers and capabilities that they themselves possess in being *their own* agents of change.

Professional development and preservice education in resilience is an opportunity to engage in the transfer of learning. Yet, to be effective, the objectives, composition, quality, and implementation of the preservice or professional development experiences focusing on the concept of resilience are imperative. The five main objectives that I articulate for the preservice and professional workshops that I provide are as follows:

1. To *inform* participants about the shift in thinking that is taking place in education, youth development, and human development. It is a shift from risk to resilience that comes from a wealth of scientific, evidence-based research and data that recognize resilience and its positive role in human development and student success.

2. To *validate* participants' wisdom, expertise, and practice in what they already know and do as qualified and experienced professionals.
3. To *connect* participants to resilience on a personal level to see how resilience has made an impact on their own lives.
4. To *empower* participants by providing them with research, tools, and strategies that support resilience and the positive outcomes that contribute to the effectiveness of believing in the capacity that all students have for resilience.
5. To *support* participants in their efforts as resilient professionals in the field of education and to facilitate their efforts to develop their own resilience support network to achieve the ultimate goal of supporting all students as whole individuals—academically, socially, emotionally, physically, and spiritually.

In Appendix B, I offer an example of a format that could be used for a preservice or professional development experience. Regardless of the format from which one ultimately chooses to work, below I discuss what I believe to be some of the most critical elements that should be incorporated into any preservice or professional development experience focused on the subject of resilience and the understanding that resilience begins with beliefs.

CRITICAL ELEMENTS

The following brief sections are just that—brief. I thoroughly recognize and honor that each topic is important enough to warrant its own book. In fact, many articles, books, and research have been done in each area and can be further explored. Yet for the purposes of this book, I want to provide a brief summary of the elements that I feel are the most important to include in any preservice or professional development experience that has the intent of influencing beliefs about student resilience.

Meeting Bio-Needs

Over my 20 years of experience of either attending professional development programs or facilitating them, I have found that meeting bio-needs that maintain levels of comfort (e.g., restroom breaks, food, movement) tops the list of things facilitators need to be attentive to. It is a matter of respect and consideration. It also falls under needs, not wants. Many professional development experiences are held after practitioners have already put in a full day's work in the classroom. Even if the whole or half day is dedicated to professional development, and those attending the professional development did not have a day of teaching, most educators will tell you that a difference in a routine (and having to be the student as opposed to the teacher) can be a difficult transition and can create different types of "energy patterns." When our energy patterns are disrupted, our bio-needs for things such as food, movement, restroom breaks, temperature control, and socializing are on a different schedule from usual. Those facilitating any professional development experience need to honor that. I often ensure that food is a part of any workshop or professional development experience and I say at the "get-go" that if people have to tend to certain "bio-needs" such as bathroom breaks or movement breaks they should please do so respectfully when the need arises. It is not my intent to hold anyone hostage.

Reframing

Reframing—moving from a deficit-based perspective to a strengths-based perspective—is at the core of the concept of resilience. In order for any of this work to be done and sustained, it is important for individuals facilitating preservice or professional development experiences on resilience do so from a strengths-based perspective and recognize that a great deal of their work is to support participants in understanding what it means to be "strengths-based"; thus modeling and offering examples of "what that looks like" is a must.

It is here that I want to convey once again that having a strengths-based perspective is not about donning rose-colored glasses. One of the comments I often hear from people who "come to the table" with a deficit mindset and are often working in a deficit-based system is something like the following: "Sounds like having a strengths-based perspective makes it sound like we all should be putting on rose-colored glasses and acting as if everything is fine and okay, and that no one should ever feel angry, depressed, or sad." This could not be further from the truth. Having a strengths-based perspective is not about forgetting, dismissing, or making light of a situation or challenge. It is not saying that everything is fine or that there is nothing to feel angry, depressed, or sad about. Having a strengths-based perspective is *all about* validating what someone is experiencing. Yet is it also about discovering, supporting, respecting, and honoring people in what they already have done to engage their resilience so that they can continue to move forward in their lives on a positive trajectory. We are not discounting feelings, emotions, trauma, and pain. What we are doing is looking at how we respond to them. Rather than responding to individuals as "victims," it is imperative to reframe and respond to them as survivors. In fact, resilience researchers Sybil Wolin and Steven J. Wolin (1999) refer to individuals who have overcome adversity as "successful survivors." They talk about successful survivors as individuals who have earned and possess a deep sense of "survivor's pride." The Wolins define survivor's pride as

rd survivor's pride

the well-deserved feeling of accomplishment that results from withstanding the pressures of hardship and prevailing in ways both large and small. It is a bitter-sweet mix of pain and triumph that is usually under the surface, but sometimes readily visible, in many children and adults struggling with the troubles in their lives. This pride, developed over time in the course of a struggle, typically goes unnoticed in professional and lay circles that are more apt to document the deficits in children than their strengths. It is not a rare feeling, nor is it limited to those with dazzling successes. Subsequent to our study, our work with youth turned up traces of survivor's pride even in young people whose struggles continued and whose hold on gratifying lives was far from sure. (p. 1)

Understanding a strengths-based perspective involves recognizing the distinction between reactions—such as anger or sadness—and responses—the ways we act in the face of such emotions. In all of this, it is always important to remember that resilience is a process. It often takes time. It often is not linear. It is riddled with challenges but also riddled with opportunities. A good way to help participants in a preservice or professional development experience find such opportunities is by understanding and engaging in the practice of reframing. And the best way to start reframing is by reflecting upon the words we use.

Words matter. Unfortunately, education is a system where all too often personal strengths get labeled in negative ways. Take, for instance, the student who may be curious and yet gets labeled distractible. Or how about the student who is passionate yet gets labeled explosive? Or the risk-taker who gets labeled rebellious? How about the introspective student who gets labeled withdrawn? Or the student with promising leadership skills who gets labeled bossy? Labels belong on soup cans, not people. When people begin to hear deficit-based labels, not only do they feel bad about themselves, but also the phenomenon of the self-fulfilling prophecy can be triggered. We can either continue taking our students down this deficit-based path or we can guide them up a healthier path.

A simple yet effective exercise that helps reframe words can be found in Appendix C. In this exercise, participants are encouraged to reframe words that describe behavior that is usually perceived as negative, challenging, or annoying, and learn to see the strengths in those behaviors and thus attribute strengths-based words to such behavior. One of my personal missions in education is to have the term *high-risk student* removed from the lexicon. It is time to recognize that students themselves are not "high risk" but rather the environments from which they come are. It may be a subtle distinction in terminology to some, but to students it is a huge distinction in how they are labeled, how they perceive themselves, and ultimately how they may engage in their education. Another "reframing mission" of mine is to have people focus as much of their attention on the "opportunity gap" as they do on the "achievement gap" when discussing the disparity in educational outcomes between groups of students. The book *Closing the Opportunity Gap: What America Must Do to Give Every Child an Even Chance* (Carter & Welner, 2013) provides a comprehensive and valuable discussion on the need to do just that.

Trust

Since people's belief systems influence and orient their practice, the nurturing and support of empathetic, compassionate, and sincere individuals who can consistently, effectively, and positively interact with children, youth, and families often reside in the ability of such individuals to continually question and challenge their own assumptions and beliefs. Thus facilitators of professional development experiences have to create and sustain safe and trusting environments for participants where humility, vulnerability, and new growth and learning will emerge, be supported, and be sustained. It's basically all about building authentic and caring relationships and creating an environment of trust—both of which take time. The type of professional development opportunity I am suggesting is not the kind that is often referred to as a "hit and run."

Much of the research about trust in education focuses on faculty trust between colleagues, trust between faculty and principal, trust between teacher and student, and trust between the teacher and the community. Building this trust takes time.

Devin Vodicka (2006), in an article about school leadership titled "The Four Elements of Trust," identifies the four elements of trust as follows: consistency, compassion, communication, and competence. For trust to emerge and be sustained, he explains, it is essential that these four elements be present together—not in isolation.

Researchers Tschannen-Moran and Hoy (1998), in their journal article "Trust in Schools: A Conceptual and Empirical Analysis," identify five key components commonly used to measure trust. These are benevolence, reliability, competence, honesty, and openness. Through my experience both as a teacher attending professional development experiences and as a presenter of many professional development topics and experiences, I have found that trust between participants and presenter is a critical element that can enhance and enrich the effectiveness of such experiences.

The cultivation and maintenance of creating trusting relationships takes a lot of foundation work. Yet I contend that it is only when administrators, educators, and others working with children, youth, and families have experienced such a trusting and respectful environment where their beliefs can be challenged, especially as they relate to the capacity for resilience, that they *then* can focus attention on what structures and approaches will best support and sustain their continued work toward positive outcomes.

Group Discussion and Professional Learning Communities (PLCs)

Group discussion and PLCs go hand in hand with the concept of trust. Sustaining a personal belief in resilience is far more likely if one is part of a supportive professional learning community. *Learning organizations* (Senge, 1990), *communities of practice* (Wenger, McDermott, & Snyder, 2002), *professional learning communities* (DuFour & Eaker, 1998; Hord, 1997), and *appreciative organizations* (Piderit, Fry, & Cooperrider, 2007) are all different terms coined for a set of transformative processes that seek to engage people in continuous learning, professional improvement, innovation, and organizational change. Pascal Kaplan (2010), founder of iCohere, a technology company dedicated to building online communities of practice and learning communities, reflects on the humanistic nature of the various approaches: "The appeal of each of these approaches is at heart a call for personal transformation, new ways of seeing, of joining with others collaboratively, setting aside older competitive, controlling and self-centered ways of interaction for the sake of shared understanding and common action for a higher good" (p. 136).

Opening yourself up to your inner beliefs is not easy. Many of us are critical enough about ourselves that we do not need to provide fodder for others to be able to criticize us. Thus a critical component in any learning environment is to create a community with a climate of mutual trust, safety, and respect. One way to do this is by taking some time as a group to collectively establish some group norms and values. These can be posted and/or discussed at the outset of any course or experience with the understanding that everyone has agreed to be respectful of them. Although every group will have its own unique norms, many groups will find that they have similar areas or topics that they address. The following brief list offers three broad areas that are usually reflected as a group develops norms:

1. *Participation.* All participants are equal and each person's voice and opinion counts.
2. *Communication.* People will speak and listen respectfully to one another without interrupting; there are no "put-downs." Members of the group will refrain from having any side conversations.
3. *Interaction.* Everyone will contribute equally. Members of the group will be respectful of beginning and ending on time.

One final comment about group norms: It is important to note that these are group norms—not ground rules. Group norms are developed together as a group whereas ground rules usually imply that they are coming from a top-down structure. Norms help facilitate effective, efficient, productive, and respectful group dynamics. Rules are restrictive. Group norms should be revisited and revised, and are unique to each group. Ground rules are seen as final, permanent, and perceived as if "one size fits all."

In an effort to further illustrate the power of group dynamics, I share a journal entry that I wrote during my research with the staff I worked with for my dissertation (Truebridge, 2010) that reflected my thoughts about the learning community that was created:

> This group has deeply established a sanctuary of sacred space. That is something we all earned and developed. There was a tone and group norm that was established. . . . What it was, was a norm and tone of speaking truths without fear, speaking truths without interruptions, speaking truths without inhibitions, speaking truths honestly, speaking truths deeply, speaking truths safely, speaking truths and being listened to and heard—not judged. These norms organically evolved and were embraced and respected and inherently understood. (p. 73)

Reflective Practices and Cognitive Dissonance

It is no surprise, and research supports, that the longer one has held on to a belief, the harder it is to change that belief (Pajares & Bengston, 1995; Prawat, 1990). Research has also demonstrated that having educators engage in reflective practices and providing them with opportunities to challenge their beliefs enhances opportunities for them to embrace, modify, influence, or alter their beliefs (e.g., Barth, 2004; Cochran-Smith, 2000; Gay & Kirkland, 2003; Johnson & Landers-Macrine, 1998; Posner, 2005; Richards, Gallo, & Renandya, 2001). This can contribute to educators being able to increase their own self-awareness and in turn being able to create classroom and school environments and climates that are conducive to enhancing student resilience and success for all.

Thoughtful and deliberate staff development and preservice experiences that introduce, discuss, and explore the concepts of resilience and beliefs benefit from having participants engage in activities and exercises that encourage and elicit reflective thinking (Schon, 1991). Such reflective thinking provides opportunities for participants to make connections, personalize, and challenge existing behaviors and beliefs. By becoming more self-aware and reflective, one is able to examine deeply held beliefs, attitudes, dispositions, and behaviors and begin to recognize how these beliefs, attitudes, dispositions, and behaviors may influence not only their practices but also the outcomes for students. Appendix D offers some questions and statements that can be used as prompts for self-reflection.

Working in the field of education is not always easy. On some days, even with the best strengths-based perspective and lens, it may be difficult to see the rewards. Then there are those other days when you know that you have made a difference in the life of a young person. Those are the days when the rewards are the most revered and comforting. Needless to say, reflecting on beliefs is not always easy and the rewards are not always immediate. Yet with persistence, the rewards of your own reflection will produce positive results in all aspects of work and life. Perhaps one of the most significant and enduring rewards of engaging in self-reflection will be that you will rediscover and tap your own natural capacity for resilience, which in turn will influence your beliefs about the natural capacity of resilience that resides in all others.

Often when I am asked what is one of the essential things that needs to happen in order for someone's beliefs to be influenced, my answer is that a person needs to experience cognitive dissonance. Being in a state of balance is comfortable. Being is a state of cognitive dissonance is a portal to growth. In 1957, psychologist Leon Festinger (1957) developed his theory on cognitive dissonance. To those in the research community, cognitive dissonance—the concept and theory—lends itself to extensive discourse and dialogue. Yet for the purpose of this book, and to understand how it is applicable in the context of teachers' beliefs about student resilience, I will abbreviate the theory as follows: Simply stated, Festinger recognized that most individuals have a deep desire to have their beliefs and behaviors aligned and in harmony. When thoughts and actions are not aligned, a feeling of disharmony and tension occurs. When this happens, individuals experience the need to alleviate such tension, which results in making an adjustment to alter their beliefs or alter their behaviors so that they are, once again, aligned and in harmony. *—Ð jʊ true!*

I use the example as I did before about how a math teacher may believe that girls are less capable than boys of learning mathematical concepts and performing mathematical computations. As a result of this thinking, the teacher's behavior may be such where the girls in the class are blatantly given less attention, called on less, and not recognized for their positive efforts. Such behavior on the teacher's part begs the question, If girls in this class are not as competent and proficient as the boys in math, is it because they are not capable or is it because they are no longer motivated because of their response to their teacher's behaviors? Right now, from the teacher's perspective, this question may not be "the issue." In the teacher's eyes, the girls are viewed as not being as capable or competent as the boys, and thus they do not warrant the same attention that the boys do. The teacher is aligning his/her behavior with his/her beliefs. Yet what if these beliefs now were to be challenged? What if that same teacher was told to "act as if" the girls were as competent and proficient in math as the boys? What if the teacher was encouraged and supported just to *try* to act differently—even though it was not consistent with his/her current belief system? What might happen?

Well, needless to say, if the girls were to respond in a positive manner, this still would not necessarily be enough to influence that particular teacher's belief systems. Perhaps, though, if getting such a positive response the first time, the teacher *continued* with such behavior—even though, mind you, it truly was inconsistent with his/her original belief system—what would happen? What may happen, and as mentioned earlier, what Thomas Guskey found in his research and what Michael Fullan discusses in his work with change, is that when a teacher alters his/her behavior in a consistent manner, which in turn elicits a consistent positive outcome from a student, such original *hard-held* beliefs can be influenced and altered. This has tremendous implications for teachers and students in terms of how teachers create the climate and culture in their classrooms and how principals create the climate and culture in their schools. Negative beliefs about factors such as students' gender, race, ethnicity, and socioeconomic status all have the potential to elicit behaviors within teachers—behaviors that may be subtle yet detrimental to the social, emotional, cognitive, and spiritual outcomes of students and their success in school in general. Resilience research consistently tells us that the three most important protective factors that mitigate and buffer risk are (1) establishing caring relationships, (2) maintaining high expectations, and (3) providing opportunities to participate and contribute. It is important for all teachers and administrators to have the opportunity for self-reflection—especially in these three areas related to fostering students' resilience—so that they can be thoughtful and aware about creating a classroom and school climate where students not only learn to their potential but also thrive. Appendix E, "Resilience in Practice Checklist: What Does It Look Like?," is a tool that can be used by teachers and administrators to further support their engagement in self-reflection in the area of the three protective factors.

Having individuals engage in reflective practices and providing them with opportunities to connect, personalize, and challenge their beliefs, particularly about students' resilience, can be incorporated into preservice and professional development experiences in a variety of ways. One way is by having participants maintain reflective journals, which are a valuable tool for the storage and transference of knowledge. The journal is a written tool with a narrative structure. Using the tool of a journal, participants reflect by reconstructing their experiences.

Participants can be asked to maintain a written journal throughout the duration of the professional development experience, providing opportunities for them to contemplate their experiences. Some entries in the journal can be at the discretion of the participants, while other entries can be guided by a question or a topic such as, When you look back upon your life, think about an experience where you felt someone believed something about you that wasn't true.

Storytelling

My dissertation, *Tell Me a Story: Influencing Educators' Beliefs about Student Resilience in an Effort to Enhance Student Success* (Truebridge, 2010), found that storytelling is a purposeful and dynamic way to reflect, construct, understand, and relate to the concept of resilience. The sharing of personal resilience stories allows participants in preservice or professional development experiences to "start where they are" as opposed to having them blindly accept what someone else, from a top-down vantage point—such as a facilitator or instructor—has to say as being true. Furthermore, it provides a platform that empowers participants to use what they already know as a vital resource for their work with others. Reflecting on one's own story of resilience helps an educator gain a deeper understanding of the concept of resilience.

Storytelling is also a powerful transformative tool. What is it about stories that makes them so powerful and transformative? An exploration into narrative theory and the understanding of the social aspect of narratives and stories helps address this question (Clandinin & Connelly, 2000; Cushing, 2006; Gubrium & Holstein, 2009).

Stories are humanizing. The power and transformative value of stories does not necessarily come from externalizing stories as much as it comes from the social interaction and analysis of the environment and the elements of the experience that occur when stories are shared. An important element that cannot be stressed enough is that the prompts and environment created for storytelling need to be driven by a resilience, strengths-based approach and perspective. This is vital to contribute to the creation of a safe and caring environment as stories are told.

There are a number of tools and strategies to draw upon to create an environment so that stories are captured from a resilience and strengths-based perspective. I use a guided visualization that is grounded in appreciative inquiry as the vehicle for setting the stage to elicit storytelling. I ask participants to visualize times in their lives when they experienced relationships, messages, or experiences that were transformative for them (see Appendix F).

After going through the guided visualization, participants are asked to use a piece of paper I have provided to them (see Appendix G) that has three prompts to assist them in identifying the environmental supports and opportunities that helped them develop their strengths. The first prompt asks them to describe or identify a transformative relationship. The second asks them to describe a transformative message that they heard. The third prompt asks them to describe a transformative opportunity or experience. In this process, participants generate their own protective factors, which almost always align with the resilience research. After participants take about 3 minutes of quiet time to jot down notes to the prompts, the telling of their stories can begin.

All participants in attendance should be given the opportunity to voluntarily share their stories. For some, this may be the first time that they will have shared such personal stories. This can become a very emotional exercise. Thus prior to the sharing of stories, facilitators of the workshop or those leading the guided visualization should always strive to create a safe, warm, and nonthreatening environment where confidences are honored. In all the years that I have done this activity, it never ceases to amaze me how generous people are with their stories and how privileged we are as participants in the same workshop to hear such stories and learn from them.

As I have alluded to earlier, storytelling allows participants to go beyond just understanding the concept of resilience; they actually connect with it. In doing so, they invariably enrich their connections with their students, as they often are able to see some similarities between themselves and their students. This quite often leads participants not only to a deeper understanding of resilience but also to a heightened level of empathy toward their students as well as others. Challenging practitioners to put into their practice what mattered to them in their lives is a powerful and effective change strategy.

Real-Life Experiences

Why would we think that educators and administrators are any different from the students in our classrooms when it comes to learning? Research continually supports the positive role that relevance has with learning. Very simply stated, motivation and learning are enhanced when we know that what we are learning has meaning in our life or that any information that is delivered in a learning environment can be integrated and applied to real-life experiences—and usually the sooner, the better.

Although teachers can be equipped with appropriate theories and beliefs about teaching and learning, they still face difficulties in implementation because the complexities and pressures of the school, classroom, and "real life" often get in the way. Ball and Cohen (1999) discuss the importance of teachers being able to learn "in and from practice rather than in preparing to practice" (p. 10).

Thus preservice and professional development experiences in education can benefit by incorporating opportunities for real-life and interactive experiences into their programs. Although preservice and professional development experiences are important venues to learn about resilience, it is just as important to recognize and remember that informal opportunities for educators and administrators to meet with their peers and discuss their real-life cases and experiences are just as valuable, and at times can have even more impact on the transfer of knowledge from one practitioner to another. Videos and DVDs illustrating best practices in resilience as well as peer observations are also effective learning tools.

Another powerful practice for bringing real-life experiences into professional development and for facilitating change in beliefs is to conduct a student fishbowl/listening circle, a highly adaptable, strengths-based process that uses basic dialogue concepts and a simple structure to encourage young people to express their opinions, ideas, and concerns about themselves and issues involving their school and education. The student fishbowl/listening circle provides practitioners with an opportunity to hear what students actually think and feel. This process has two requirements: (1) a set of agreements that all will honor and respect and (2) an appreciative inquiry approach.

Appreciative inquiry was developed by David Cooperrider and Suresh Srivasta in 1980 (Watkins & Mohr, 2001). It is based on the premise that organizations and systems such as education and schools should be built around what works as opposed to looking to fix what doesn't. Appreciative inquiry is a process that reframes one's thinking and actions from being deficit based to strengths based. Engaging stakeholders in appreciating what is best in themselves, as the student fishbowl/listening circle exercise does, leads to the identification of what is positive and creates a positive and energetic atmosphere of collaboration among all stakeholders in finding ways to get there. Unfortunately, individuals and processes that focus on problems continue in a vortex of negative thinking that ultimately keeps individuals and organizations in a place of dysfunction.

As part of this strengths-based activity, students agree to reframe their complaints and issues as suggestions and recommendations for change. The process of conducting a student fishbowl/listening circle is discussed in Appendix H.

Inviting participants to share their own personal real-life resilience stories is also a powerful tool for influencing beliefs. It only takes one person who rises above the trauma, adversity, and challenge that practitioners see in their students' lives every day to show that resilience is indeed possible. The guided imagery exercise mentioned in the previous section is a good tool to use here as well.

Research

Educators are professionals who are lifelong learners. They need to be respected and honored as such. There is a constant discussion in education about creating a bridge between research and practice. The only way, though, that a bridge between research and practice can truly be made and can be effective is if research by the academy is shared with the community of practitioners, and the practices of those in the trenches are shared with researchers in academia. Unfortunately, this is not often the case. Tension, instead of communication, is what so often exists today between the two communities of research and practice. In a refreshing article in *Educational Researcher*, David E. Labaree (2008), a professor in the School of Education at Stanford, comments about another article that references bridging research to practice and reframes this existing tension as an opportunity "to enrich both modes of professional practice" (p. 422).

Research on any topic of professional development—even the topic of professional development itself—can be found, disseminated, and critically discussed among participants in an educational preservice class or a professional development experience. With the work I do, I integrate the research that has been done on the topic of resilience—especially as it relates to education. In terms of the sharing of resilience research, some individuals prefer to have more research than others. Summaries of existing research, with the proper citations available for obtaining the original research, are appropriate ways to disseminate certain types of research. Appendix I provides an example of how the research from the often-cited longitudinal resilience study done by Werner and Smith has been summarized. (This seminal resilience research is often referred to as the Kauai Longitudinal Study.)

As I mentioned earlier, I have made a concerted effort to provide extensive references throughout this book so that those reading and working with it can extend their inquiry, knowledge, and research in an area that may be of particular interest to them. It is also important for me to provide references to research because research empowers educators as they make decisions on what practices to bring into their classrooms.

Parallel Process

Personal resilience, teacher resilience, and student resilience are all intertwined. Furthermore, the resilience of a school or district depends on the attitudes, beliefs, and dispositions of individuals working throughout them as well. In education, the ability to embrace a resilience perspective needs to be supported through a parallel process that provides professional development growth opportunities on all levels—not just for practitioners but also for principals, support staff (including counselors, nurses, custodians, and bus drivers), and all staff at the district level. It is essential that any educational preservice or professional development experience on resilience include a parallel process whereby educational practitioners, administrators, and staff are provided with ample opportunities to engage in an understanding and awareness of positive human development and their *own* capacity for resilience. The importance of "taking care of the caretaker" is imperative and cannot be emphasized enough. I often use the "oxygen mask in an airplane" metaphor to illustrate this point.

Cultural Responsiveness

Different cultures embrace different perspectives and values that are often embedded in such activities as traditions, childrearing, boundaries, and achievement. Thus it is crucial that all individuals working in education develop an understanding and appreciation of resilience within a cultural context. In any preservice or professional development experience dealing with resilience, participants need to spend some time understanding the concept of cultural responsiveness. Geneva Gay (2002) defines culturally responsive teaching "as using the cultural characteristics, experiences, and perspectives of ethnically diverse students as conduits for teaching them more effectively" (p. 106). Educators need to be purposeful and draw from the cultures and values of the students and families they are working with rather than imposing specific curriculum materials, behaviors of communication, and educational interventions and strategies based on the dominant culture, which in fact may not be reflected in their school or classroom. Therefore participants in a preservice or professional development experience need to be supported in being culturally responsive in their discussions about resilience, selection of curriculum materials, communication and interaction with parents and the community, choice of educational interventions and strategies, and all other aspects of their work. That said, the only way to know if you are truly being culturally responsive is to check out your assumptions with the individuals you are serving. It is all too easy to assume, for example, that all individuals of any one culture or group have the same values. There is individual variation within all cultures and groups. If you really listen to your students and families, they will tell you how you can best support them.

The National Center for Culturally Responsive Educational Systems (NCCRESt) (www.nccrest.org), EdChange (www.edchange.org), Teaching Tolerance (www.tolerance.org), and In Time (www.intime.uni.edu/multiculture/) are all good resources for information on cultural responsiveness.

POSSIBLE/SUGGESTED FORMAT

As mentioned earlier, the format for a preservice or professional development course or experience reinforcing the understanding that resilience begins with beliefs is offered in Appendix B. This format follows the process identified in the conceptual framework. The preservice and/or professional development course activities can include videos, small- and large-group discussions, student fishbowl/listening circles, personal reflection, and reflective journal writing. When designing the format for the preservice or professional development experience that will be used for educational practitioners, administrators, and staff, it is important to note that it should be designed to accommodate *their* schedules and needs. The structure and time frame for designing and implementing the preservice or professional development experience should continually be evaluated with input from participants with regard to its efficiency and effectiveness.

Appenix B is an example of a professional development format that I have used to bring the concept and practice of resilience to practitioners in education. Modifications and adaptations are always necessary so that each format and experience is inclusive and respectful of the unique features of everyone involved—the teachers, administrators, and staff; the families and students they serve; and the community in which they all live and work.

This particular format was developed around the theme "You Matter!" (Benard, Burgoa, & Truebridge, 2007). Its theme reflects the message that every person in human services and education has the power to make a difference in the lives of others. This professional development experience is implemented as a series with three 2-hour modules. The duration between sessions should be determined so participants are able to adequately practice and reflect upon some of the strategies presented.

Reflection Section

1. Some of the main concepts, ideas, tools, and/or strategies I learned from this chapter include _____.

2. A personal experience that allows me to relate to the concepts, ideas, tools, and/or strategies presented in the chapter occurred

   _____.

3. An example of how I have used or will use the concepts, ideas, tools, and/or strategies presented in the chapter in my current practice is

   _____.

4. In my future practice I would like to build upon the concepts, ideas, tools, and/or strategies presented in the chapter by

   _____.

5. Ways in which I may need more information, resources, or support to further an understanding or implementation of the concepts, ideas, tools, and/or strategies presented in the chapter are

   _____.

6. A question I still have about the concepts, ideas, tools, and/or strategies presented in the chapter is _____.

CHAPTER 6

Sustaining Resilience in Your School, Students, and Self

> I quote others only in order the better to express myself.
>
> —Michel de Montaigne

> I love quotations because it is a joy to find thoughts one might have, beautifully expressed with much authority by someone recognized wiser than oneself.
>
> —Marlene Dietrich

In many of the workshops I facilitate and the speaking opportunities that I have, I get the chance to share some of my favorite quotes. More often than not, these quotes seem to be able to capture and convey a thought, feeling, or aspect in a way that is much more powerful than any words I could articulate. Invariably, at the end of my workshop or speaking engagement, I am approached by people who ask about the quotes and want to write them down so they can reflect on them some more or share them with a colleague or friend.

I purposefully chose to include a substantial number of quotes in this book not to fill for content but rather to fill one's heart and soul. Many of the quotes I have collected are ones that are especially good at conveying some final thoughts about sustaining resilience in your school, students, and self. I invite readers to take the time to read and reflect on the following quotes, especially in the context of the heading under which each falls. Whether you use this book for your own purposes or in the context of a class, group-work, or professional learning community, these quotes lend themselves as prompts for journaling, discussions, and further reflections and queries centered around influencing educators' beliefs about student resilience in an effort to enhance student success.

TAPPING YOUR OWN RESILIENCE: AN IMPORTANT FIRST STEP

One of the best ways to help individuals understand the concept of resilience is to have them connect personally with it. As mentioned in Chapter 5, using guided imagery is an effective way to make this connection.

Guided imagery activities conducted as part of a preservice or professional development experience ask participants to visualize times in their lives when they experienced relationships, messages, or activities that were transformative for them. Challenging participants to put into their practice what mattered to them in their lives is a powerful and effective learning tool as well as an effective mechanism to influence change in their beliefs and practices.

> *When I do not know myself, I cannot know who my students are. I will see them through a glass darkly, in the shadows of my unexamined life—and when I cannot see them clearly, I cannot teach them well.*
> —Parker Palmer, *The Courage to Teach: Exploring the Inner Landscape of a Teacher's Life*

> *The greatest magnifying glasses in the world are a man's own eyes when they look upon his own person.*
> —Alexander Pope

> *The real man smiles in trouble, gathers strength from distress, and grows brave by reflection.*
> —Thomas Paine

WORDS MATTER

What's in a word? TONS! Words are powerful and we must never underestimate how our words, our tone, and our body language can impact others. Paula Denton (2007), in her book *The Power of Our Words*, draws upon the work of Russian psychologist Lev Vygotsky. In *Mind in Society*, Vygotsky (1978) reminds us that language produces "fundamentally new forms of behavior" (p. 24). Hence, language goes beyond the simple expression of thoughts, feelings, and experiences—language actually shapes them.

The words and language we hear about ourselves from others often influences who we are now, how we perceive ourselves to be today, and how we dream about becoming in the future. As we all know, words can have a negative effect as well as a positive one. Unfortunately, and all too often, children and youth are the recipients of negative words and language. Such words and language become difficult things to overcome as they sometimes stick like labels on a soup can. Having the capacity to be resilient, hearing positive messages that are authentic and sincere, and replacing negative narratives with positive ones—which includes the negative narratives we hear from others as well as the ones that play in our own heads—can get us beyond the negative labels, stereotypes, and words people have inflicted upon us and move us in a direction to grow, develop, and thrive as healthy individuals.

> *The language we use shapes the way we think. We cannot change our attitudes and actions until we change our words.*
> —Karen Hall, Syracuse Cultural Workers 2000 Calendar

> *Kind words can be short and easy to speak, but their echoes are truly endless.*
> —Mother Teresa

> *A torn jacket is soon mended; but hard words bruise the heart of a child.*
> —Henry Wadsworth Longfellow

> *Of all the powerful weapons of destruction that man could invent, the most terrible—and the most powerful—was the word. Daggers and spears left traces of blood; arrows could be seen at a distance. Poisons were detected in the end and avoided . . . but the word managed to destroy without leaving clues.*
> —Paulo Coelho

THE SILVER LINING OF ADVERSITY

Challenging life experiences and events can be opportunities for growth, development, and change. Quite often, our perseverance through tough times builds our confidence and makes us stronger. Michael Rutter (2012) talks about a "steeling effect" whereby successful coping with stress or adversity can lead to improved functioning and increased resistance to stress or adversity.

*You gain strength, and courage, and confidence by every
experience in which you really stop to look fear in the face . . .
you must do the thing you think you cannot do.*
—Eleanor Roosevelt

*Difficulties give us the opportunity to prove our greatness by
overcoming them.*
—Meher Baba

*One who gains strength by overcoming obstacles possesses the
only strength which can overcome adversity.*
—Albert Schweitzer

*To accomplish great things we must not only act, but also dream;
not only plan, but also believe.*
—Anatole France

*If you will call your troubles experiences, and remember that
every experience develops some latent force within you, you will
grow vigorous and happy, however adverse your circumstances
may seem to be.*
—John Heywood

TAKE CARE OF THE CARETAKER

Educators, as well as any individuals working in human services, cannot dismiss the value of taking care of the caretaker. As I mentioned in the preceding chapter, well-designed and well-implemented preservice and professional development experiences on resilience need to also engage in a parallel process whereby participants are provided and supported with a working understanding and awareness of human development and resilience in themselves. They need a working environment that fosters and nurtures their resilience—one that provides authentic caring relationships, maintains appropriate high expectations, and provides meaningful opportunities for participation and contribution.

*When we truly care for ourselves, it becomes possible to care far
more profoundly about other people. The more alert and sensitive
we are to our own needs, the more loving and generous we can be
toward others.*
—Eda LeShan

To *create these places and to be that "someone," we must, first
and foremost, support our own resilience.*
—Bonnie Benard, "The Foundations of the Resiliency Paradigm"

*Systems change when groups of people together tap their resilience
and change from the inside out.*
—Kathy Marshall, National Resilience Resource Center

THE POWER OF ONE

Somewhere along the education road we took a wrong turn and lost our direction. Somewhere along the way we began to convince ourselves that education is only about what is in our heads. What we forgot is that it is more
than that. Education is as much about our hearts as it is about our heads.

Perhaps the wrong turn in education happened when too many people
believed that there was a distinct separation between emotion and cogni-
tion. Yet that distinction no longer exists as research, especially brain research, is finding what teachers for centuries already knew: Emotion and
learning are not only related, but also, and more often than not, emotions
are portals for increased motivation and cognitive functioning.

This knowledge has important implications in education—especially in
terms of the potent connection and relationship between the teacher and the
student. Yes, once again, it is about connections and relationships.

In doing my research, I have asked people what they remember most
about their schooling. Most people respond and speak from the heart and
share a memory of one teacher—one teacher who made a difference in
their life.

There is no shortage of books today with stories about how one teacher
has made a difference in the life of a student. Sometimes these stories are
incredibly dramatic—other times they are very subtle. And that is what we
all need to remember. In this world of instant gratification, you may have
no idea how you may have touched a student's heart and soul. But what
that student will never forget in that moment and for the rest of his or her
life, is that you did. "The Starfish Story" at the end of this section is a lovely
parable that can be used in any setting or workshop to convey this poignant
message.

So often in education we talk about the potential of our students. What
we also need to focus on is the potential, not to mention the power and
privilege, that we have to be that one adult that will connect with a student's
heart and soul to make a difference in that student's education and life. Researcher and Stanford professor Nel Noddings, in a 1988 *Education Week*

article titled "Schools Face Crisis in Caring" states, "My guess is that when schools focus on what really matters in life, the cognitive ends we now pursue so painfully and artificially will be achieved somewhat more naturally. . . . It is obvious that children will work harder and do things—even odd things like adding fractions—for people they love and trust" (p. 32).

Yes, we have gone astray in education, but it is not too late to get on the right path. To do so, though, we must reorient ourselves. This means getting out of our heads and getting back in touch with our hearts. If this sounds a bit counterintuitive, do some research on your own. Talk to a teacher, or better yet, talk to a student.

> *Those of us who are in this world to educate—to care for—young children have a special calling: a calling that has very little to do with the collection of expensive possessions but has a lot to do with worth inside of heads and hearts.*
> —Fred M. Rogers

> *As so many of us have personally experienced, the actions of significant individuals—perhaps a teacher who came our way at just the right time—helped instill self-beliefs that influence the course and direction our lives take.*
> —Frank Pajares, interview, quoted in Madewell & Shaughnessy

> *Shifting the balance or tipping the scales from vulnerable to resiliency may happen as a result of one person or one opportunity . . . one family member, one teacher, one school, one community person . . .*
> —Bonnie Benard

> *I am only one, but still I am one; I cannot do everything, but still I can do something; and because I cannot do everything I will not refuse to do the something that I can do.*
> —Edward Hale

> *One looks back with appreciation to the brilliant teachers, but with gratitude to those who touched our human feelings. The curriculum is so much necessary raw material, but warmth is the vital element for the growing plant and for the soul of the child.*
> —Carl Jung

> *A teacher affects eternity; he can never tell where his influence stops.*
> —Henry Adams

→ LOVE this ☺

The Starfish Story

An old man was picking objects off the beach and tossing them out into the sea. A young boy approached him and saw that the objects were starfish.

"Why in the world are you throwing starfish into the water?" he asked.

"Well you see, the tide has gone out and if all these the starfish are still on the beach when the sun rises high in the sky, they will die," replied the old man.

"That is ridiculous. There are thousands of miles of beach and millions of starfish. You can't really believe that what you are doing could possibly make a difference!" quipped the young boy.

The old man picked up another starfish, paused thoughtfully, and remarked as he tossed it out into the waves:

"It makes a difference to this one."

—Adapted from Loren Eiseley

IT BEGINS WITH BELIEFS

Research and literature support the claim that the theory of resilience begins with beliefs. Providing people who work with children and youth with opportunities to understand the theory of resilience coupled with opportunities to reflect upon their own beliefs, especially how they pertain to student resilience, is a positive step as one works in the field of education.

What the mind can conceive and believe, and the heart desire, you can achieve.

—Norman Vincent Peale

 Perhaps I am stronger than I think.

—Thomas Merton

A teacher must believe in the value and interest of his subject as a doctor believes in health.

—Gilbert Highet

Every great dream begins with a dreamer. Always remember, you have within you the strength, the patience, and the passion to reach for the stars to change the world.

—Harriet Tubman

All action results from thought, so it is thoughts that matter.

—Sai Baba

Reflection Section

1. Some of the main concepts, ideas, tools, and/or strategies I learned from this chapter include _____.

2. A personal experience that allows me to relate to the concepts, ideas, tools, and/or strategies presented in the chapter occurred

    _____.

3. An example of how I have used or will use the concepts, ideas, tools, and/or strategies presented in the chapter in my current practice is_____.

4. In my future practice I would like to build upon the concepts, ideas, tools, and/or strategies presented in the chapter by

    _____.

5. Ways in which I may need more information, resources, or support to further an understanding or implementation of the concepts, ideas, tools, and/or strategies presented in the chapter are

    _____.

6. A question I still have about the concepts, ideas, tools, and/or strategies presented in the chapter is _____.

Conclusion

In the conclusion of her book *Resiliency: What We Have Learned*, Bonnie Benard (2004) asks about the steps ahead in the work of resilience and youth development: "What must we provide for youth, and for those who work with them? How can we have the most effect? And what challenges must we address?" She suggests, "We need to begin with belief in the innate resilience of every human being" (p. 386). Embracing this suggestion and noting in my Introduction that one of the recurring messages in resilience research posits the relationship that beliefs have with resilience—resilience begins with what one believes—I began my research wanting to explore how one might influence such beliefs. My quest to do so led me to recognize a void in the literature. There was scant, if any, resilience research or literature that specifically discussed how beliefs about resilience or specifically student resilience could be influenced. At the same time, a review of literature on beliefs and professional development in disciplines connected with human services suggested that specific types of professional development could, in fact, influence beliefs. What I found missing once again was the specificity of research or literature connecting professional development with influencing the beliefs specifically of student resilience.

Research supports the importance of studying beliefs in the context of education because beliefs influence the behaviors of educational practitioners, which in turn influence the behaviors and success of their students. Resilience research supports the argument that discussions about education reform and transformation cannot be limited to discussions about *best practices* as reflected in curriculum and programs. Such best practices are only as good as the practitioners who are able to implement them with their pedagogical best practices, thus creating educational climates and cultures conducive to student learning. As Walsh (1997) states, "When there's improvement, it usually isn't that the services *per se* were different, it's about a change in the person who delivered the service, and the way they delivered it" (p. 7).

Research suggests that positive educational climates and cultures in classrooms and schools promote student engagement, motivation, and self-efficacy, which in turn increase student success. Resilience research has identified specific strategies that educators can incorporate into their practice to enhance the environmental conditions in classrooms and schools.

Given the important role that educational environments have in enhancing student success, stakeholders in education would benefit from examining how a teacher's understanding and belief in student resilience is developed, nurtured, and sustained. With such an understanding, all stakeholders in education would be motivated to do what they could to ensure that they contributed to an educational environment rich in protective factors. When educational policies and schools themselves create learning opportunities that incorporate the protective factors, they are tapping into students' intrinsic motivational drives, and students become engaged in learning. It is time to acknowledge that among the greatest barriers to student learning are educational policies and practices that ignore human cognitive, psychological, neurological, and biological functioning. Conversely, the greatest support to student learning that education systems can provide—without any cost—is the creation of policies and practices that are grounded in this understanding of how students are motivated to learn.

Now is the time to recognize and address the fact that the most positive learning environments for our students are those where we believe in the resilience of all our students and are able to provide them with the developmental support and opportunities that they need to be successful in school and beyond. Providing educational practitioners, administrators, and school staff with opportunities to reflect upon their beliefs, especially how they pertain to student resilience, is a positive first step in the goal of improving student success for all.

Epilogue

In many ways, my story and my journey began with beliefs and continue with beliefs. Working in policy, I wholeheartedly believed in the resilience of the education system—its components: the schools, the teachers, the students, and parents—as well as the system itself. As a teacher, I intuitively believed in the resilience of all of my students. As a researcher, I methodically built upon the previous resilience research and cognitively believed the claim that the theory of resilience begins with beliefs. Having resided in education policy, practice, and research, I am comfortable navigating the complicated labyrinth we often call our education system. I am also comfortable interpreting the jargon between the three worlds in an effort to support a shared vision with shared outcomes. Yet regardless of my vocation or whether I situate myself in research, policy, or practice, today or tomorrow, I will always combine these three perspectives under the umbrella and role of the eternal and optimistic advocate for children, youth, and education. We must never lose sight that the true focus of education should be on the student—the whole student. As an advocate, I will continue to believe in my head, heart, and soul that education reform focusing solely on spending more money to alter programs and curriculum is often misdirected. Integrated throughout this belief is my notion that when we use semantics and refer to making changes in education as "education reform," we often are compelled to look at the parts of education that are believed to be in need of improvement. I contend that it is time we reframed the needs in education by altering semantics and saying that the education system is in need of "education transformation." With this perspective, teachers, administrators, policymakers, parents, and students may more readily embrace a "theory of change" in education where the change agent resides not *with the programs* incorporated in the system, but rather *within the individuals* creating and implementing the system.

Personal Resilience Strengths

These are examples of internal resources and supports that can both promote resilience and manifest as a result of resilience.

Social: Social Competence

- *Responsiveness:* Is attentive and quick to react in situations
- *Flexibility:* Adjusts and adapts to change without force
- *Cultural Responsiveness:* Is able to learn from and relate respectfully to people from one's own culture and other cultures
- *Empathy:* Has the ability to connect and understand the feelings of another; is able to "walk in someone else's shoes"
- *Caring:* Provides sincere and authentic interest, compassion, and concern
- *Communication Skills:* Is able to clearly impart thoughts, information, and/or opinions either by writing, talking, or using another form of transmission
- *Sense of Humor:* Has the ability to laugh and be amused at oneself and in response to difficult situations

Emotional: Autonomy

- *Positive Identity:* Feels good about oneself and who he or she is
- *Self-Efficacy:* Maintains a belief in one's own power and abilit79y to succeed in certain situations
- *Initiative:* Takes on things before being asked to do something; is motivated to act without being told to act
- *Mastery:* Possesses great skill or knowledge in a specific area
- *Self-Awareness:* Is aware of one's own feelings, character, strengths, and challenges

Cognitive: Problem Solving

- *Planning:* Has the ability to create a process or procedure ahead of time for carrying out a goal

- *Seeking Alternatives:* Is curious and searches for different ways of doing or seeing things
- *Critical Thinking:* Is able to skillfully conceptualize, analyze, synthesize, and evaluate information
- *Resourcefulness:* Is capable of finding ways and means of addressing, responding, and being attentive in a variety of situations, especially new and difficult ones

Moral/Spiritual: Sense of Purpose and Future

- *Connectedness:* Has the sense of belonging and being connected to something greater than oneself (e.g., others, nature, earth)
- *Goal Directedness:* Has a purpose
- *Imagination:* Has a creative mind to think of things that are not always based in reality
- *Aspirations:* Has a strong desire, longing, ambition, or aim to achieve something
- *A Special Interest/Hobby:* Engages in an activity outside of one's vocation for the purpose of joy, pleasure, and/or relaxation
- *Persistence:* Is able to stick to something and continue and focus on something even in difficult situations; "stick-to-itiveness"
- *Optimism:* Maintains a positive and favorable attitude and looks on the bright side of events or situations
- *Faith:* Has an unwavering belief and trust in something or someone
- *Sense of Meaning:* Has an understanding of one's significance, purpose, and/or existence in life

Source: Appendix A was adapted from materials used by Bonnie Benard in her resilience training and workshops.

Possible/Suggested Format for a Preservice/Professional Development Experience

One suggested format for reinforcing the understanding that resilience begins with beliefs would be to divide the preservice or professional development experience into three modules. The following information provides a brief overview of each module.

Module 1

Participants learn the major messages and contributions of resilience and research, the personal strengths associated with resilience, and how to use strengths-based approaches in their work with students. Activities may include

1. Emphasizing the power of words and the need to reframe "deficit" language as strengths-based language, for example, *hyperactive* versus *energetic*, *distractible* versus *curious*, and *explosive* versus *passionate*.
2. Making connections with their own resilience by reflecting on personal stories that demonstrate their internal personal strengths.
3. *Homework:* Practice using strengths-based language in your classroom/school and personal life.

Module 2

Participants learn how the protective factors of caring relationships, high expectations, and opportunities for participation meet the needs of students and families. Activities may include

1. Engaging in a guided imagery exercise to explore and identify the effect that caring relationships, high expectations, and opportunities to participate had on their personal lives.

2. Reviewing the resilience conceptual framework.
3. Watching a video of best practices in action and identifying when there are real-life examples of caring relationships, high expectations, and opportunities to participate.
4. *Homework:* Engage in a self-reflection activity and identify times at work when you fostered caring relationships, high expectations, and opportunities to participate among the students and families with whom you work.

Module 3

Participants engage in personal reflection and dialogue about their practices and attitudes in providing and conveying the three protective factors to their students. Participants learn the significance of collegial support in supporting resilience practices. Activities may include

1. Engaging in role-plays using strengths-based communication and reframing, especially with difficult situations that might occur with students, families, or colleagues.
2. Dialoguing about how resilience begins with our beliefs—that resilience starts with us and the beliefs we have in our hearts about not only the individuals and families with whom we work, but also our own resilience.
3. Identifying what you need from your colleagues to support your own resilience beliefs.
4. Publicly committing to one strengths-based practice to support your students' resilience, one to support your colleagues', and one to support your own.

Source: Benard & Truebridge, 2013.

Reframing:
From Deficit-Based
Words to Strengths-Based Words

Participants—either alone, in small groups, or all together—are invited to read the deficit-based word on the left, visualize the behavior that is associated with that word, and then come up with a word that is strengths-based to describe that same behavior that the student is manifesting.

Deficits	Strengths
Hyperactive	
Impulsive	
Stubborn	
Willful	
Tests Limits	
Explosive	
Defiant	
Angry	
Manipulative	
Disorganized	
Withdrawn	
Aggressive	
Noncommunicative	
Victim	

Source: Adapted from Phillips, 2011.

Self-Reflection: Questions and Statements to Reflect Upon and Discuss

- What is standard English?
- Do you have different opinions when you see four African American or Hispanic male teens in the school hallway versus four White male teens?
- What is the difference between a group and a gang? Between being assertive and aggressive?
- Two consecutive years of bad teaching could destroy a child for life.
- A child has a much greater chance of being placed in special education or tracked in remedial classes if he or she doesn't look or speak like the teacher.
- The ideal student is one who can sit still for long periods of time, quietly working by him/herself.
- School is the first place where most children learn how to fail.
- One of the best ways to evaluate a school is by the conversation in the teachers' lounge.
- If we believe all children can learn, then why do so many adults accept studies describing the plight of low-income, fatherless, African American children?
- Do schools educate, level, track, or miseducate?
- Is different synonymous with deficient?
- Schools reward incompetence.
- Would you, as a teacher, teach differently if your own child were in your classroom? Explain.
- Schools can be defined as "at-risk environments" for some children and youth.

- Are educators only trained to teach motivated students?
- When schools retain students but do not change teachers' expectations, time on task, pedagogy, or curriculum but expect better results, it borders on insanity.
- In low-income schools, good behavior is valued more than learning.
- Attention deficit disorder (ADD) and attention deficit hyperactivity disorder (ADHD) has been around ever since teachers have attempted to instruct students on issues in which they have no interest. It should be defined as a teaching disability rather than a learning disability.

Source: Adapted from Kunjufu, 2002.

Resilience in Practice Checklist: What Does It Look Like?

This is a tool that can be used by teachers and staff at all grades and levels: classroom, school, and district.

Place a plus sign by the items already being implemented. Place a check mark by the ones you would like to improve or strengthen.

Challenge yourself: For each item listed, try to go "one step further" by asking, "What does this look like?" For instance, when reading "Models empathy and compassion," ask yourself, "What does this look like?" Keep breaking it down to the most concrete examples and strategies you can come up with.

CARING RELATIONSHIPS

Classroom

___ Creates and sustains a caring climate

___ Models empathy and compassion

___ Aims to meet developmental needs for belonging and respect

___ Is available/responsive

___ Offers extra individualized help

___ Ensures a commitment to being culturally responsive

___ Gets to know the life context of students

___ Has long-term commitment

___ Actively listens

___ Shows common courtesy

___ Respects others

___ Uses appropriate self-disclosure

___ Pays personal attention

___ Shows interest

___ Checks in

___ Gets to know hopes and dreams

___ Gets to know interests

___ Shows respect for and acknowledges students' feelings

___ Apologizes when mistakes are made

___ Names and accepts students' feelings

___ Is nonjudgmental

___ Looks beneath "challenging" behavior

___ Reaches beyond the resistance

___ Uses humor/smiles/laughter

___ Is flexible

___ Shows patience

___ Uses community-building process

___ Creates small, personalized groups

___ Creates opportunities for peer-helping

___ Uses cross-age mentors (older students, family/
community members)

___ Creates connections to resources:

    ___ Education

    ___ Culture

    ___ Employment

    ___ Service

    ___ Recreation

    ___ Health, counseling, and social services

___ Builds a sense of community in the classroom that is committed to
all students being invited, valued, included, and having a voice

___ Makes sure body gestures convey intentions
(e.g., smiles, eye contact, nods)

___ Keeps an open-door policy with students and family (If need
be, select a specific time/day when you can be reached.)

___ Makes accommodations for interpreters if language is an issue
during meetings

___ Learns the names of all students and how to pronounce names properly

___ Makes personal contact with students every day—
something as simple as a hello or a smile

___ Sets up peer support networks in the classroom to help new students and
families acclimatize and be aware of all services/programs available to them

___ Talks with students to see how they access care/support (Share what is
being done in your grade, subject, or area with the rest of the school.)

___ Takes time to chat with students outside the classroom

School

___ Builds a sense of community in the school that is committed to all students,
    families, and staff being invited, valued, included, and having a voice

___ Creates small groups of staff who can work as
    a team to be available to students

___ Engages students, staff, and parents in a school climate
    survey that includes protective factors

___ Makes sure that the principal and other adults are available to
    students by having an open-door policy where students feel
    comfortable dropping in if they need help or just want to talk

___ Creates a school climate task force consisting of students,
    teachers, and other adults in the school, and parents who
    continually assess the quality of the school environment

___ Creates focus groups of teachers and other adult staff to explore ways for
    making the school climate and policies more supportive of their work

___ Acts on teacher recommendations

___ Conducts student fishbowl/listening circle experiences
    and invites parents and community members

___ Creates a master calendar/schedule for subject/departmental tests and projects
    so as to eliminate multiple tests/projects being done on the same days

___ Institutes mentoring opportunities for teachers, other adults in the school,
    older high school and college students, and community volunteers

___ Organizes schoolwide retreats

___ Organizes teacher support groups

___ Provides new teacher mentoring

___ Continues to read resilience research and literature

___ Sets up peer support networks in the school to help new students and families
    acclimatize and be aware of all services/programs available to them

___ Shares success stories and gives updates on resilience
    research and literature during staff meetings

___ Thanks administrators and staff often for implementing
    strategies to minimize disruptions

___ Respects, values, and supports the resilience of all staff

District

___ Builds a sense of community in the district that is committed to all students,
    families, and staff being invited, valued, included, and having a voice

___ Visits schools and classrooms regularly

___ Engages in a school climate survey for students, staff,
    and parents that includes protective factors

___ Analyzes issues/challenges to see if there are patterns

___ Creates districtwide staff support groups

___ Creates mentoring programs that connect community adults to
students in the school—increasing substantially the number of adults
in the community who learn about young people's lives and their
challenges as well as youths' incredible strengths and capacities

___ Develops a central schedule for selected meetings

___ Develops district policies on interruptions

___ Educates school community and district personnel about the
protective role of caring relationships and why attention to
supporting the "care of the caretaker" is important

___ Circulates success stories

___ Invites community volunteers to read to students in the classrooms

___ Reduces the adult-student ratio through cooperative learning and
inviting in older peer helpers, family, and community volunteers

___ Seeks input from other sites or districts to see
their solutions to similar challenges

___ Creates "dialogue nights" where adults and youth can talk
together in an atmosphere of mutual trust and safety

___ Conducts student fishbowl/listening circle experiences
and invites parents and community members

___ Hosts parent information sessions, varying the times to accommodate
all parents (Not all adults are comfortable in a school setting, so
consider hosting events in other places other than the school, e.g.,
community centers, faith-based centers, small gatherings at homes.)

___ Seeks a community-liaison volunteer to enhance and maintain a
positive relationship between the school and the community

___ Respects, values, and supports the resilience of
colleagues and educators in the district

HIGH EXPECTATIONS

Classroom

___ Sustains a high-expectation climate honoring each student's unique strengths

___ Conveys "no excuses, never give up" philosophy
(grit, persistence, determination)

___ Models and teaches that mistakes and setbacks are opportunities for learning

___ Provides descriptive and timely feedback to students about their work

___ Recognizes progress as well as performance

___ Aims to meet developmental needs for mastery, challenge, and meaning

___ Believes in innate capacity of all to learn

___ Sees students as vital partners in school improvement

___ Focuses on the whole child (social, emotional, cognitive, physical, spiritual)

___ Understands the needs motivating student behavior and learning

___ Sees culture as an asset

___ Challenges and supports ("You can do it"; "I'll be there to help.")

___ Connects learning to students' interests, strengths,
     learning styles, experiences, dreams, and goals

___ Provides appropriate wait time after questions for thinking and responding

___ Encourages creativity and imagination

___ Asks open-ended questions that encourage students to
     interpret, analyze, synthesize, and evaluate

___ Uses a variety of assessments and evaluations,
     including formative and summative ones

___ Conveys hope and optimism

___ Affirms/encourages the best in students

___ Attributes the best possible motive to behavior

___ Articulates clear expectations/boundaries/structure

___ Provides clear explanations

___ Holds students accountable

___ Models boundary-setting

___ Uses management and discipline that is consistent and fair

___ Models and teaches adaptive distancing and conflict resolution

___ Uses rituals and traditions

___ Recognizes strengths and interests

___ Mirrors strengths and interests

___ Uses strengths and interests to address concerns/challenges

___ Employs authentic assessment

___ Groups students heterogeneously

___ Continuously challenges "isms"—e.g., racism,
     sexism, ageism, classism, homophobia

___ Helps to reframe self-image from "at-risk" to "at-promise"

___ Helps to reframe problems and challenges as opportunities

___ Conveys messages to students that they all have the capacity for resilience

___ Sees students as constructors of their own knowledge and meaning

___ Teaches critical analysis/consciousness

___ Encourages mindfulness and self-awareness of moods, thinking, and actions

___ Relates to family and community members with high expectations

___ Calls home/communicates with home to report
     students' good behavior and achievements

___ Helps family members see students' strengths, interests, and goals

School

___ Challenges the myths held about certain groups of children, youth, and families

___ Focuses on curriculum that is thematic, experiential, challenging, comprehensive, and inclusive of multiple perspectives

___ Groups students heterogeneously, promoting cooperation, shared responsibility, and a sense of belonging

___ Provides training in resilience, youth development, and assets to help change deeply held beliefs about students' capacities

___ Provides training on supports and accommodations

___ Shares success stories and gives updates on resilience research and literature during staff meetings

___ Models the language of success to all students

___ Encourages and supports the resilience of all staff

District

___ Focuses instruction on a broad range of learning styles and multiple intelligences that builds from student strengths, interests, and experiences

___ Utilizes authentic and formative assessments

___ Encourages and supports self-reflection

___ Continues to read education research through a critical lens with the understanding of what constitutes "good and valid" research

___ Questions how success is defined in education and in the district

___ Gathers data on other indicators of success—not just standardized test scores

___ Visits schools and classrooms regularly

___ Ensures a commitment to being culturally responsive

MEANINGFUL PARTICIPATION AND CONTRIBUTION

Classroom

___ Builds a democratic, inclusive community

___ Practices equity and inclusion

___ Aims to meet developmental needs for power, autonomy, meaning, and so on

___ Provides opportunities for voice

___ Provides opportunities for decisionmaking

___ Provides opportunities for problem solving

___ Empowers students to create classroom norms/agreements

___ Is aware of being culturally responsive and creating a classroom that is culturally responsive

___ Holds daily and as-needed class meetings

___ Gives youth meaningful roles and responsibilities

___ Infuses communication skills into all learning experiences

___ Creates opportunities for creative expression
   ___ Art
   ___ Music
   ___ Writing/Poetry
   ___ Storytelling/Drama
   ___ Other
___ Provides opportunities for students to use/contribute their
   ___ Strengths and interests
   ___ Goals and dreams
___ Includes and engages marginalized groups
   ___ Girls/Women
   ___ Students of color
   ___ Students with special needs
   ___ Other
___ Infuses service learning into the program/curriculum
___ Infuses active learning and project-based learning into the program/curriculum
___ Uses cooperative learning
___ Uses adventure/outdoor experience-based learning
___ Offers peer-helping
___ Offers cross-age helping
___ Provides ongoing opportunities for personal reflection
___ Provides ongoing opportunities for dialogue/discussion
___ Uses small, interest-based groups
___ Uses restorative justice in place of punitive discipline
___ Engages students—especially those on the margin—
   in a school climate improvement task force
___ Invites the participation and contribution of family and community
   members in meaningful classroom activities (not just cooking/baking)
___ Builds a sense of community in the classroom that is committed to all
   students and families being invited, valued, included, and having a voice
___ Ensures ALL students are included in class activities
   and are aware of extracurricular activities
___ Asks questions that encourage self-reflection, critical thinking, and dialogue
___ Asks students their opinions on issues and classroom challenges
___ Engages in technology support training
___ Engages students in setting their own goals
___ Gives students more opportunities and time to respond to questions
___ Makes learning more "hands on"
___ Seeks training opportunities to work effectively with families and staff

School

___ Builds a sense of community in the school that is committed to all students, families, and staff being invited, valued, included, and having a voice

___ Engages in a school climate survey for students, staff, and parents that includes protective factors

___ Ensures that all students and families have information and access to all school activities

___ Documents the effectiveness of new alternatives and ideas that are implemented

___ Encourages community groups to be involved in school, including involvement with physical activity and health promotion

___ Engages students—especially those who may be on the margin—in a school climate improvement task force

___ Establishes peer-helping/tutoring and cross-age mentoring/tutoring programs

___ Expands/continues to expand collaboration within the school community, including students

___ Holds meetings with key stakeholders to review strategies for coordinating meetings and paperwork

___ Provides information to all students and families about access to school counseling and support; finds out why perhaps they haven't been taking part and plans around the issues, e.g., time schedule issues, language issues, lack of prior experience, financial issues

___ Provides nutritional information and alcohol and substance abuse education materials in multiple languages for parents/guardians as well as students

___ Provides time, venue, and agenda for staff collaboration

___ Raises issues at staff meetings and allows for productive and positive brainstorming sessions on alternatives that include all staff

___ Reads resilience research and literature

___ Shares success stories and gives updates on resilience research and literature during staff meetings

___ Sets up peer support networks in the classroom/school to help new students and families acclimate to the new environment

___ Supports, promotes, and expects collaboration between special education and general education

___ Uses focus groups to ascertain why a group is not involved in some/all activities (Possible reasons may include awareness, time, money, transportation.)

District

___ Builds a sense of community in the district that is committed to all students,
    families, and staff being invited, valued, included, and having a voice
___ Engages in a school climate survey for students, staff,
    and parents that includes protective factors
___ Engages students in a neighborhood mapping project in an effort
    to identify pro-youth resources, services, and facilities
___ Visits schools and classrooms regularly
___ Addresses teaming/collaboration
___ Creates environments for dialogue between adults and youth where
    they can talk together in an atmosphere of mutual trust and safety
___ Develops policy guidelines to reduce interruptions
___ Forms youth advocacy groups around policy issues such as mental health,
    physical health, and safety, and gives students the opportunity to examine local
    ordinances so that they can learn how to become advocates in systemic change
___ Provides information to all students and families about access to mental
    health care and other services; finds out why perhaps they haven't
    been taking part and plans around the issues, e.g., time schedule
    issues, language issues, lack of prior experience, financial issues
___ Promotes success stories to a wider audience using social media
___ Seeks a community-liaison officer/volunteer to enhance
    communication, cooperation, and understanding
___ Seeks input from other school sites and districts (regions/state)
    regarding how challenges and issues are resolved/alleviated

SELF-REFLECTION

Once time has been spent on the checklists, the next step would be to engage in a self-reflection exercise around the protective factors.

Caring Relationships

List examples of your strengths in providing caring relationships:

_____

_____

_____

List challenges you want to work on:

_____

_____

_____

High Expectations

List examples of your strengths in providing high expectations:

_____

_____

_____

List challenges you want to work on:

_____

_____

_____

Opportunities for Participation and Contribution

List examples of your strengths in providing opportunities for participation and contribution:

_____

_____

_____

List challenges you want to work on:

_____

_____

_____

Source: Appendix E was adapted from materials used by Bonnie Benard in her resilience training and workshops.

Guided Visualization: Personal Reflection— Facilitator's Reading

Facilitator reads the following script (the ellipses indicate pauses):

Close your eyes, take a deep breath . . .

Let's take a minute to think back over your growing up—anytime from childhood on to adolescence and young adulthood . . .

Think about what needs, what deep longings you had, what callings of your heart . . .

Create a mental image of your younger self . . .

Now think about a person who was "there" for you . . . who helped guide you . . . someone who contributed to your sense of self . . . who supported you in meeting your life's challenges . . . who helped you recognize your strengths, your inner power . . . someone who fostered your resilience . . .

Maybe this person didn't appear in childhood; that's okay. Think of someone later in your life who made a difference for you. Create a mental image of this person . . . think of some words that describe *how* this person was with you.

Now think about some messages that this person—or others—gave you . . . what did she/he or they say or express to you . . . what messages did you receive about yourself, about who you were . . . who you are as a person . . . your capabilities . . . your strengths . . . what you did or do well . . . messages about your inner power to overcome adversities . . . what messages supported you in meeting the challenges of your life . . . what messages fostered your resilience, helped you see yourself in a new way . . .

Now turn your attention to the opportunities and experiences that helped you become who you are now, opportunities and experiences that helped you see and develop your strengths and capabilities . . . that helped you meet your life's challenges . . . picture one or two opportunities and experiences that maybe changed your life course in some way . . . that fostered your resilience, that helped you see yourself and your life in a new way . . . that helped you realize your power to overcome.

Let's breathe with these thoughts for just a minute, taking a deep breath and then letting it go easily . . . and one more breath. Now open your eyes, focusing on one point in front of you and then coming back into the room . . . bring yourself—your strengths, your power, your relationships, messages, and opportunities and experiences—back into the room with you . . .

After taking participants through the guided visualization, say:

> Now take just a couple of minutes and using the Guided Visualization handout for participant's notes (Appendix G), do a "quick write"—jot down what came up for you during this guided imagery. Identify who was there providing you with a transformative relationship and specifically think of some words that describe *how* this person was with you. Then describe the transformative messages and the opportunities and experiences that fostered your resilience.

Next, share personal stories in small groups, giving everyone the right to "pass."

Source: Appendix F was adapted from materials used by Bonnie Benard in her resilience training and workshops.

Guided Visualization: Personal Reflection— Participant's Notes

Take a few minutes to think back over your growing up and identify what environmental and developmental supports and opportunities helped you develop your personal strengths.

Describe a

1. Caring Relationship

Who was the person and what relationship did they have with you?

_____

_____

_____

What words describe *how* this person was with you and how did they show they cared?

_____

_____

_____

2. Message of High Expectations

What were some of the positive messages people said that supported you during times of adversity or stress?

_____

_____

_____

3. Opportunity to Participate and Contribute

What things did you do or what experiences/opportunities did someone provide for you that made you feel good about what you were doing and good about yourself?

_____

_____

_____

Source: Appendix G was adapted from materials used by Bonnie Benard in her resilience training and workshops.

Conducting a Student Fishbowl/ Listening Circle

The student fishbowl/listening circle is a highly adaptable, strengths-based process that uses basic dialogue concepts and a simple structure to encourage young people to express their opinions, ideas, and concerns about themselves and issues involving their school and education. The purpose is to provide an opportunity for adults to hear what young people need from them to be healthy and successful. As a strengths-based process, it is important that the questions *not* be asked in the context of "what is wrong" but rather be asked in the context of what is needed from adults and schools so that they—the youth—can be healthy and successful.

The reversal of formal roles, where young people speak and adults listen, makes a strong impression on young people and adults alike. Youth take the role very seriously and appreciate the opportunity to speak about what is important to them. The youth learn that young people of different backgrounds have very similar perspectives on many important questions and they develop greater respect for both their similarities and their differences. The adults learn that youth understand a great deal about themselves and their educational environment and that youth value the adults who genuinely want to help them. The young people have realistic ideas about changes that can be made to make schools and education better and are willing to share responsibility for making changes happen. The adults and youth in partnership develop strategies for change that will make a clear difference and begin to strengthen adult/youth relations. The youth fishbowl focus group process is being used successfully with youth of all ages to improve their health, education, schools, and communities.

LISTENING CIRCLE GUIDELINES

Youth

- Should represent the program, school, and so on as a whole (all ethnic, racial, social, and cultural groups, abilities, and levels of success).
- Serve as participant researchers.

Adults

- Watch, listen, and take notes, but do not speak.
- There is no direct interaction between the youth and the adult observers during the listening group.

Listening Circle Agreements

Youth agree to

- Turn off cell phones/no texting.
- Focus on what they do like/want/need.
- Only use names for positive comments.
- Be respectful of each other.
- Remember time limitations.
- Speak their truth!

Adults agree to

- Turn off cell phones/no texting.
- Stay for the entire listening circle.
- Be silent during the listening circle.
- Keep the comments offered by youth anonymous (except for mandatory reporting).
- Commit to a plan of action that reflects the young people's perspectives.

BEFORE THE LISTENING CIRCLE SESSION

Introductions

Before the listening circle begins, the adult facilitator meets with the youth as a group and welcomes the young people, introduces him/herself, and asks the youth to introduce themselves to each other and write their first names on their name badges. The adult facilitator then gives an overview of the listening circle process, stresses how important their ideas are, and reassures the young people that their specific comments are to be kept confidential. The facilitator presents the Youth Agreements and asks for any other agreements they need for this to be a safe and comfortable process. Four to six questions, printed on separate and differently colored cards (index cards are good to use), are distributed and explained to the youth. Ample time is given so that they may write their responses to each question on the cards and ask for any clarification. Writing their responses helps the young people keep track of their thoughts while others are speaking during the listening circle process. Having each question on a different-colored card also helps to keep things organized (e.g., blue for question 1, yellow for question 2). This preliminary process is best done away from the adult observers in a separate, quiet room.

DURING THE LISTENING CIRCLE SESSION

Seating

The youth should be seated in a circle with the adults sitting around them in a larger circle, fishbowl style.

Welcome

The facilitator welcomes the adults, explains the process, asks if they can agree to the Adult Agreements, and reminds them that their role is to listen to the young people. No one should be let in or out of the room during the session and all cell phones should be turned off. The youth then go around the circle and introduce themselves by first name only. If appropriate, grade level, school site, and so forth may be added.

Asking Questions

No more than six questions should be asked, one at a time, for the group to answer. As each question is asked, the facilitator calls on one youth at a time, going around the circle in order. The process continues with one person at a time answering the same question. (The facilitator can start with a different person each time.) After everyone has had an opportunity to offer a response, the facilitator asks youth participants if there are any additional ideas that have not been expressed. After all questions have been asked, if there is adequate time the facilitator may ask additional questions to clarify or obtain more detailed information.

Closure

The facilitator thanks the young people for their participation and contribution and invites them to be involved in any planning process that will result because of the focus group information. While the adults are still there, the youth should be asked to express their feelings on the experience of being formally listened to by the adults. The adults should also be asked to express their feelings on the experience of listening. The adults may ask the youth clarifying questions at this time.

NEXT STEP: YOUTH DEVELOPMENT PLANNING

The planning session begins with a dialogue about the themes and key points made by the youth. Once the concerns and recommendations of the young people have been identified, the discussion should identify possible resolutions that reflect the youth responses. The youth should be invited to participate in the planning, and should be asked for clarification details and their recommendations for solutions. Next steps should be identified and responsibilities assigned. If youth have *not* been invited to participate in this planning process, the recommended next steps should be presented to them for their feedback. Creating a structure for ongoing youth involvement in program improvement is also a task of this planning group.

Program/Public Announcement

Some form of public announcement should be made to confirm the changes that will be made as a result of the youth listening circle process.

Suggested Questions to Ask the Students
(It is recommended that you limit the number of questions to six.)

1. What does it mean to be a successful student here? What are your teachers and school doing to help you?
2. What needs to happen to make your school a more caring place? We'd like to hear some specific examples and suggestions.
3. How do you know when an adult believes in you? What do they say or do?
4. What would make school more fun, interesting, and less stressful for you and your friends?
5. What would you like to do in school?
6. Have you ever been asked about what you thought of school or education? Who has asked and what have they asked?
7. What kinds of decisions would you like to make in your classrooms, schools, and about your education?
8. What do you think is the very best thing about your school?
9. When you think about how things have changed here in the past school year, what positive changes come to mind? Are there more changes that would help and support you?
10. What are your dreams, hopes, goals, and aspirations? Are there adults who know them? What do you need from the adults in your school, home, or community to help you achieve your goals and dreams?

Source: Adapted from Network of Regional Educational Laboratories, 2000.

The Kauai Longitudinal Study: Emmy Werner and Ruth Smith

The bullet points provide a summary of the study.

- Developmental longitudinal research: birth to adulthood (evaluated at 1, 2, 10, 18, 32, and 40 years of age).
- Began with nearly 700 children born in 1955 on the Hawaiian island of Kauai.
- About one-third of infants born that year were identified as "high risk" and had at least one (usually more) of these four risk factors: poverty, parental psychopathology (included alcohol abuse), parental conflict, and perinatal stress (e.g., low birth weight, born prematurely).
- One out of three identified as "high risk" grew into "a competent, confident, and caring young adult by age 18" (Werner & Smith, 1992, p. 2).
- By age 40 "not one of these individuals was unemployed, none had been in trouble with the law, and none had to rely on social services. Their divorce rates, mortality rates and rates of chronic health problems were significantly lower at midlife than those of their same sex peers" (Werner, 2005, p. 12).
- Study identified not only the individual strengths that helped this cohort "make it" but also the nature of the environmental supports and opportunities that facilitated the development of these strengths and noninvolvement in negative behaviors.
- Findings indicated that many in the high-risk cohort experienced positive turning points in their 20s and 30s, indicating that early events in the life of children from high-risk environments are not the only avenues to positively affect later adjustment.

Werner and Smith (1992) state:

> Our findings and those by other American and European investigators with a life-span perspective suggest that these buffers [protective factors] make a more profound impact on the life course of children who grow up under adverse conditions than do specific risk factors or stressful live events. They appear to transcend ethnic, social class, geographical, and historical boundaries. Most of all, they offer us a more optimistic outlook than the perspective that can be gleaned from the literature on the negative consequences of perinatal trauma, caregiving deficits, and chronic poverty. They provide us with a corrective lens—an awareness of the self-righting tendencies that move children toward normal adult development under all but the most persistent adverse circumstances. (p. 202)

NOTE

Refer to the following materials for more information:

Werner, E. (2005). Resilience and recovery: Findings from the Kauai Longitudinal Study. *Focal Point: Research, Policy, and Practice in Children's Mental Health, 19*. Available at pathwaysrtc.pdx.edu/focalpointS05.shtml

Werner, E., & Smith, R. (1992). *Overcoming the odds: High-risk children from birth to adulthood.* Ithaca, NY: Cornell University Press.

Processing the Process and Action Planning

This is a tool that can be used at the end of a class or a professional development experience. Consider all the information that you have read and discussed. Use these questions and statements as prompts to help you incorporate what you have read and discussed about resilience and beliefs into your work, assignments, responsibilities, research, and so on.

Processing the Process

1. What does this work look like to make it feel like it is making a difference?
    - To you
    - In your classroom
    - In your school
    - In the district
    - To students
    - To parents
    - To the community
    - Other

2. What does success look like?
    - To you
    - In your classroom
    - In your school
    - In the district
    - To students
    - To parents
    - To the community
    - Other

3. What will you do with all of this information?
    - Individually
    - As a group
    - As a school
    - As a district
    - Other

Short- and Long-Term Action Planning

1. Activities/ideas/research I want to accomplish include _____.
2. Starting tomorrow I will _____.
3. During the next 2 weeks, I will _____.
4. During the next month, I will _____.
5. During the next year, I will _____.
6. Ways in which I need resources and support are _____.
7. A question I still have is _____.

References

Abeles, V. (Producer & Codirector). (2009). *Race to nowhere* [Motion picture]. La-fayette, CA: Reel Link Films, www.racetonowhere.com.

Agne, K. J., Greenwood, G. E., & Miller, L. D. (1994). Relationships between teach-er belief systems and teacher effectiveness. *The Journal of Research and Devel-opment in Education, 27,* 141–152.

Akcy, T. M. (2006). *Student context, student attitudes and behavior, and academic achievement: An exploratory analysis.* New York: Manpower Development Re-search Corporation.

Andrews, R. L., Soder, R., & Jacoby, D. (1986). *Principal roles, other in-school variables, and academic achievement by ethnicity and SES.* Paper presented at the annual meeting of the American Educational Research Association (AERA), San Francisco, CA.

Ball, D. L., & Cohen, D. K. (1999). Developing practice, developing practitioners: Toward a practice-based theory of professional education. In G. Sykes & L. Darling-Hammond (Eds.), *Teaching as the learning profession: Handbook of policy and practice* (pp. 3–32). San Francisco: Jossey-Bass.

Bamburg, J. D. (1994). *Raising expectations to improve student learning.* Urban monograph series. (ERIC document ED 378290)

Bandura, A. (1993). Perceived self-efficacy in cognitive development and function-ing. *Educational Psychologist, 28,* 117–148.

Barth, R. S. (2004). *Learning by heart.* San Francisco: Jossey-Bass.

Behar, L. S., Pajares, F., & George, P. S. (1996). The effect of teachers' beliefs on students' academic performance during curriculum innovation. *High School Journal, 79,* 324–332.

Benard, B. (1986). Characteristics of effective prevention programs. *Prevention Fo-rum, 6*(4), 3–8.

Benard, B. (1991). *Fostering resiliency in kids: Protective factors in the family, school and community.* Portland, OR: Western Center for Drug-Free Schools and Communities.

Benard, B. (1993, March). Resiliency requires changing hearts and minds. *Western Center News, 6,* pp. 5–6.

Benard, B. (1999). The foundations of the resiliency paradigm. In N. Henderson, B. Benard, & N. Sharp-Light (Eds.), *Practical ideas for overcoming risks and building strengths in youth, families, & communities* (p. 8). San Diego, CA: Resiliency in Action.

Benard, B. (2003). Turnaround teachers and schools. In B. Williams (Ed.), *Closing the achievement gap* (2nd ed., pp. 115–137). Alexandria, VA: Association for Supervision and Curriculum Development.

Benard, B. (2004). *Resiliency: What we have learned.* San Francisco, CA: WestEd.

Benard, B., Burgoa, C., & Truebridge, S. (2007). *You matter! The power of after school program staff to make a difference in the lives of children and youth.* Training and materials prepared in accordance with a California Department of Education grant awarded to WestEd.

Benard, B., & Marshall, K. (1997, Spring). A framework for practice: Tapping innate resilience. *Research/Practice. 5.* Available at www.cehd.umn.edu/Search/default.html?query=tapping+innate&Search.x=0&Search.y=0

Benard, B., & Truebridge, S. (2013). A shift in thinking: Influencing social workers' beliefs about individual and family resilience in an effort to enhance well-being and success for all. In D. Saleebey (Ed.), *The Strengths perspective in social work practice* (6th ed., pp. 201–219). Upper Saddle River, NJ: Pearson.

Bronfenbrenner, U. (1979). *The ecology of human development: Experiments by nature and design.* Cambridge, MA: Harvard University Press.

Brooks, R., & Goldstein, S. (2001). *Raising resilient children.* Chicago: Contemporary Books.

Brooks, R., & Goldstein, S. (2003). *Nurturing resilience in our children.* Chicago: Contemporary Books.

Brooks, R., & Goldstein, S. (2004). *The power of resilience: Achieving balance, confidence, and personal strength in your life.* Chicago: Contemporary Books.

Brophy, J., & Evertson, C. (1981). *Student characteristics and teaching.* New York: Longman.

Brophy, J., & Good, T. (1970). Teachers' communication of differential expectations for children's classroom performance: Some behavioral data. *Journal of Educational Psychology, 61,* 365–374.

Brown, J., D'Emidio-Caston, M., & Benard, B. (2001). *Resilience education.* Thousand Oaks, CA: Corwin Press.

Brownell, M. T., & Pajares, F. M. (1996). The influence of teachers' efficacy beliefs on perceived success in mainstreaming students with learning and behavior problems: A path analysis. *Florida Educational Research Council Research Bulletin, 27* (3–4), 11–24. (ERIC Document Reproduction Service No. ED409661)

Carter, P. L., & Welner, K. G. (Eds.). (2013). *Closing the opportunity gap: What America must do to give every child an even chance.* New York: Oxford University Press.

Cefai, C. (2008). *Promoting resilience in the classroom: A guide to developing pupils' emotional and cognitive skills.* Philadelphia, PA: Jessica Kingsley Publishers.

Center on the Developing Child, Harvard University. *Toxic stress: The facts.* Available at developingchild.harvard.edu/topics/science_of_early_childhood/toxic_stress_resp

Clandinin, J., & Connelly, F. M. (1987). Teachers' personal knowledge: What counts as 'personal' in studies of the personal. *Journal of Curriculum Studies, 19*, 487–500.

Clandinin, J., & Connelly, F. M. (2000). *Narrative inquiry: Experience and story in qualitative research*. San Francisco: Jossey-Bass.

Cochran-Smith, M. (2000). Blind vision: Unlearning racism in teacher education. *Harvard Educational Review, 70*, 157–190.

Combs, A. (1988). New assumptions for educational reform. *Educational Leadership, 45*, 38–40.

Committee on Integrating the Science of Early Childhood Development. (2000). *From neurons to neighborhoods: The science of early childhood development*. (J. P. Shonkoff & D. A. Phillips, Eds.). Washington, DC: National Academy Press.

Cuban, L. (1995). The hidden variable: How organizations influence teacher responses to secondary science curriculum reform. *Theory Into Practice, 34*, 4–11.

Cushing, P. (2006). (Story-)Telling it like it is: How narratives teach. In V. Raoul, C. Canam, A. D. Henderson, & C. Paterson (Eds.), *Unfitting stories: Narrative approaches to disease, disability, and trauma*. Waterloo, ON: Wilfred Laurier Press.

Cushman, K. (2003). *Fires in the bathroom: Advice for teachers from high school students*. New York: The New Press.

Cushman, K. (2005). *Sent to the principal: Students talk about making high schools better*. Providence, RI: Next Generation Press.

Dary, T., & Pickeral, T. (Eds.). (2013). *School climate: Practices for implementation and sustainability*. A School Climate Practice Brief, Number 1. New York: National School Climate Center.

Davis, D. M. (Ed.). (2007). *Resiliency reconsidered: Policy implications of the resiliency movement*. Charlotte, NC: Information Age Publishing.

Davis, S. H. (2007). Bridging the gap between research and practice: What's good, what's bad, and how can one be sure? *Phi Delta Kappan, 88*, 569–578.

De La Ossa, P. (2005). "Hear my voice": Alternative high school students' perceptions and implications for school change. *American Secondary Education, 34*, 24–39.

Denton, P. (2007). *The power of our words*. Turners Falls, MA: Northeast Foundation for Children.

DuFour, R., & Eaker, R. (1998). *Professional learning communities at work: Best practices for enhancing student achievement*. Bloomington, ID: Solution Tree Press.

Dweck, C. S. (2006). *Mindset*. New York: Random House.

Eccles, J. S., & Wigfield, A. (2002). Motivational beliefs, values, goals. *Annual Review of Psychology, 53*, 109–132.

Fang, Z. (1996). A review of research on teacher beliefs and practices. *Educational Research, 38*, 47–65.

Fenstermacher, G. D. (1979). A philosophical consideration of recent research on teacher effectiveness. In L. S. Shulman (Ed.), *Review of research in education* (Vol. 6, pp.157–185). Itasca, IL: Peacock.

Ferguson, R. F. (2003). Teachers' perceptions and expectations and the Black-White test score gap. *Urban Education, 38,* 460–507.

Festinger, L. (1957). *A theory of cognitive dissonance.* Evanston, IL: Row, Peterson.

Feuerstein, R., Feuerstein, R. S., & Falik, L. H. (2010). *Beyond smarter: Mediated learning and the brain's capacity for change.* New York: Teachers College Press.

Fullan, M. (2008). *The six secrets of change.* San Francisco: Jossey-Bass.

Garmezy, N. (1987). Stress, competence, and development: Continuities in the study of schizophrenic adults, children vulnerable to psychopathology, and the search for stress-resistant children. *American Journal of Orthopsychiatry, 57,* 159–174.

Garmezy, N., & Masten, A. S. (1986). Stress, competence, and resilience: Common frontiers for therapist and psychopathologist. *Behavior Therapy, 17,* 500–521.

Garmezy, N., & M. Rutter, M. (Eds.). (1983). *Stress, coping, and development in children.* New York: McGraw-Hill.

Gay, G. (2002). Preparing for culturally responsive teaching. *Journal of Teacher Education, 53,* 106–116.

Gay, G., & Kirkland, K., (2003). Developing cultural critical consciousness and self-reflection in preservice teacher education. *Theory Into Practice, 42,* 181–187.

Ginott, H. G. (1972). *Teacher and child.* New York: Macmillan.

Glantz, M., & Johnson, J. (Eds.). (1999). *Resilience and development: Positive life adaptations.* New York: Kluwer Academic/Plenum Publishers.

Goddard, R. D. (2003). The impact of schools on teacher beliefs, influence, and student achievement. In J. Rath & A.C. McAninch (Eds.), *Teacher beliefs and classroom performance: The impact of teacher education: Vol. 6. Advances in teacher education* (pp. 183–202). Greenwich, CT: Information Age Publishing.

Goldstein, S., & Brooks, R. (Eds.). (2005). *Handbook of resilience in children.* New York: Kluwer Academic/Plenum Publishers.

Goleman, D. (1995). *Emotional intelligence: Why it can matter more than IQ for character, health and lifelong achievement.* New York: Bantam Books.

Greenberg, M. (2006). Promoting resilience in children and youth. In B. M. Lester, A. S. Masten, & B. McEwen (Vol. Eds.), *Annals of the New York Academy of Sciences: Vol. 1094. Resilience in children* (pp. 139–150). Malden, MA: Blackwell Publishing.

Gubrium, J. F., & Holstein, J. A. (2009). *Analyzing narrative reality.* Thousand Oaks, CA: Sage Publishing, Inc.

Guskey, T. R. (1986). Staff development and the process of teacher change. *Educational Researcher, 15,* 5–12.

Gutman, L. M., Sameroff, A. J., & Cole, R. (2003). Academic growth curve trajectories from 1st grade to 12th grade: Effects of multiple social risk factors and preschool child factors. *Developmental Psychology, 39,* 777–790.

Hall, G., & Hord, S. (2006). *Implementing change: Patterns, principles, and potholes* (3rd ed.). Boston: Pearson Education, Inc.

Halpern, R. (2004). *Confronting the big lie: The need to reframe expectations of afterschool programs.* Paper commissioned by Partnership for After School Programs, New York.

Henderson, N., & Milstein, M. M. (2003). *Resiliency in schools.* Thousand Oaks, CA: Corwin Press.

Higgins, G. O. (1994). *Resilient adults: Overcoming a cruel past.* San Francisco: Jossey-Bass.

Hollingsworth, S. (1989). Prior beliefs and cognitive change in learning to teach. *American Educational Research Journal, 26,* 160–189.

Hong, Y., Dweck, C., Chiu, C., Lin, D. M.-S., & Wan, W. (1999). Implicit theories, attributions, and coping: A meaning system approach. *Journal of Personality and Social Psychology, 77,* 588–599.

Hord, S. (1997). *Professional learning communities: Communities of continuous inquiry and improvement.* Available at eric.ed.gov:80/ERICDocs/data/eric-docs2sql/content_storage_01/0000019b/80/14/24.pdf

Hughes, M. (1995). *Achieving despite adversity: Why are some schools successful in spite of the obstacles they face? A study of the characteristics of effective and less effective elementary schools in West Virginia using qualitative and quantitative methods.* Charleston, WV: West Virginia Education Fund.

Jackson, Y. (2011). *The pedagogy of confidence: Inspiring high intellectual performance in urban schools.* New York: Teachers College Press.

Jessor, R. (1993). Successful adolescent development among youth in high-risk settings. *American Psychologist, 48,* 117–126.

Johnson, V. G., & Landers-Macrine, S. (1998). Student teachers explain changes in their thinking. *The Teacher Educator, 34,* 30–40.

Jussim, L. (1986). Self-fulfilling prophecies: A theoretical and integrative review. *Psychological Review, 93,* 429–445.

Kagan, D. M. (1992). Implications of research on teacher belief. *Educational Psychologist, 27,* 65–90.

Kaplan, H. (1999). Toward an understanding of resilience: A critical review of definitions and models. In M. D. Glantz & J. L. Johnson (Eds.), *Resilience and development: Positive life adaptations* (pp. 17–83). New York: Kluwer Academic/Plenum Publishers.

Kaplan, P. (2010). The learning communities of 2020. In V. Washington & J. D. Andrews (Eds.), *Children of 2020: Creating a better tomorrow* (p. 136). Washington, DC: Council for Professional Recognition and National Association for the Education of Young Children

Krovetz, M. (1999). *Fostering resiliency.* Thousand Oaks, CA: Corwin Press.

Kunjufu, J. (2002). *Black students—Middle class teachers.* Chicago: African American Images.

Labaree, D. F. (2008). The dysfunctional pursuit of relevance in education research. *Educational Researcher, 37,* 421–423.

La Cerra, P., & Bingham, R. (2002). *Origin of minds.* New York: Harmony Books.

Lawrence, S. M., & Tatum, B. D. (1997). Teachers in transition: The impact of antiracist professional development on classroom practice. *Teachers College Record, 99,* 162–178.

Lerner, R. M. (2006). Resilience as an attribute of the developmental system: Comments on the papers of Professors Masten & Wachs. In B. M. Lester, A. S. Masten, & B. McEwen (Vol. Eds.), *Annals of the New York Academy of Sciences: Vol. 1094. Resilience in children* (pp. 40–51). Malden, MA: Blackwell Publishing.

Lester, B. M., Masten, A. S., & McEwen, B. (Eds.). (2006). *Resilience in children. Annals of the New York Academy of Sciences* (Vol. 1094). Malden, MA: Blackwell Publishing.

Love, A. (2003, April). *The measurement of teachers' beliefs as cultural context for successful learning of African American children.* Paper presented at the annual meeting of the American Educational Research Association, Chicago, IL.

Love, N. (2000). Beliefs that block equity. Available at lscnet.terc.edu/do.cfm/paper/8247/show/use_set-culture

Luthar, S. S. (2006). Resilience in development: A synthesis of research across five decades. In D. Cicchetti & D. J. Cohen (Eds.), *Developmental psychopathology: Risk, disorder, and adaptation* (2nd ed., pp. 739–795). New York: Wiley.

Luthar, S. S., Barkin, S. H., & Crossman, E. J. (In press). "I can, therefore I must": Fragility in the upper-middle classes. *Development and Psychopathology, 25th Anniversary Special Issue.*

Luthar, S. S., & Cicchetti, D. (2000). The construct of resilience: Implications for interventions and social policies. *Development and Psychopathology, 12,* 857–885.

Luthar, S. S., Cicchetti, D., & Becker, B. (2000a). The construct of resilience: A critical evaluation and guidelines for future research. *Child Development, 71,* 543–562.

Luthar, S. S., Cicchetti, D., & Becker, B. (2000b). Research on resilience: Response to commentaries. *Child Development, 71,* 573–575.

Luthar, S. S., Sawyer, J. A., & Brown, P. J, (2006). Conceptual issues in studies of resilience: Past, present, and future research. In B. M. Lester, A. S. Masten, & B. McEwen (Vol. Eds.), *Annals of the New York Academy of Sciences: Vol. 1094. Resilience in children* (pp. 105–115). Malden, MA: Blackwell Publishing.

Madewell, J., & Shaughnessy, M. F. (2003). An interview with Frank Pajares. *Educational Psychology Review, 15,* 375.

Maslow, A. (1943). A theory of human motivation. *Psychological Review, 50,* 370–396. Available at psychclassics.yorku.ca/Maslow/motivation.htm

Masten, A. S. (1994). Resilience in individual development: Successful adaptation despite risk and adversity. In M. C. Wang & E. W. Gordon (Eds.), *Educational resilience in inner-city America: Challenges and prospects* (pp. 3–25). Hillsdale, NJ: Erlbaum.

Masten, A. S. (1997). Resilience in children at-risk. University of Minnesota, Center for applied research and educational improvement, *Research/Practice, 5,* Number 1.

Masten, A. S. (2001). Ordinary magic: Resilience processes in development. *American Psychologist, 56,* 227–238.

Masten, A. S., & Obradovic, J. (2006). Competence and resilience in development. In B. M. Lester, A. S. Masten, & B. McEwen (Vol. Eds.), *Annals of the New York Academy of Sciences: Vol. 1094. Resilience in children* (pp. 1–12). Malden, MA: Blackwell Publishing.

Mayo Clinic Staff. (2010). Stress: Constant stress puts your health at risk. Available at www.mayoclinic.com/health/stress/SR00001

McDonald, F., & Elias, P. (1976). *The effects of teaching performance on pupil learning, Vol. I: Beginning teacher evaluation study, Phase 2.* Princeton, NJ: Educational Testing Service.

Merriam-Webster's Online Dictionary. (2009). Influence. Available at www.merriam-wwebster.com/dictionary/influence

Merton, R. K. (1968). *Social theory and social structure.* New York: Free Press.

Munby, H. (1982). The place of teachers' beliefs in research on teacher thinking and decision making, and alternative methodology. *Instructional Science, 11,* 201–225.

National Research Council and the Institute of Medicine. (2004). *Engaging schools: Fostering high school students' motivation to learn.* Committee on Increasing High School Students' Engagement and Motivation to Learn. Board on Children, Youth, and Families, Division of Behavioral a Social Sciences and Education. Washington, DC: National Academies Press.

Nespor, J. (1987). The role of beliefs in the practice of teaching. *Journal of Curriculum Studies, 19,* 317–328.

Network of Regional Educational Laboratories. (2000). *Listening to student voices: Self-study toolkit.* Portland, OR: Northwest Regional Educational Laboratory.

New York Times. (2012). Can school performance be measured fairly? [Opinion Pages: Room for Debate]. Available at www.nytimes.com/roomfordebate/2012/07/29/can-school-performance-be-measured-fairly/?nl=todaysheadlines&emc=thab1_20120730

Nichols, S. L., & Berliner, D. C. (2007). *Collateral damage: How high-stakes testing corrupts America's schools.* Boston: Harvard Education Press.

No Child Left Behind (NCLB) Act of 2001, Pub. L. No. 107-110, § 115, Stat. 1425 (2002).

Noddings, N. (1988, December 7). Schools face crisis in caring. *Education Week, 8* (14), 32.

Noddings, N. (2003). *Happiness and education.* New York: Cambridge University Press.

Norgaard, J. M. (2005, February). *The measurement of attribution of battering: A review of the literature.* Available at www.ceu-hours.com/courses/battering.html

Obiakor, F. E. (2000). *Transforming teaching-learning to improve student achievement.* Paper presented at the Best Practice Conference, Institute for the Transformation of Learning, Marquette University, Milwaukee, WI.

Olson, K. (2009). *Wounded by school: Recapturing the joy in learning and standing up to old school culture.* New York: Teachers College Press.

Pajares, F. (1992). Teachers' beliefs and educational research: Cleaning up a messy construct. *Review of Educational Research, 62,* 307–332.

Pajares, F. (1993). Preservice teachers' beliefs: A focus for teacher education. *Action in Teacher Education, 15,* 45–54.

Pajares, F. (1996). Self-efficacy beliefs in academic settings. *Review of Educational Research, 66,* 543–579.

Pajares, F. (2000, January). *Schooling in America: Myths, mixed messages, and good intentions.* Lecture delivered at Emory University, Atlanta, GA.

Pajares, F., & Bengston, J. K. (1995). *The psychologizing of teacher education: Formalist thinking and preservice teachers' beliefs.* Paper presented at the meeting of the American Educational Research Association, San Francisco.

Palmer, P. (1998). *The courage to teach: Exploring the inner landscape of a teacher's life.* San Francisco: Jossey-Bass.

Perry, B. D. (2002). How children become resilient. *Scholastic Parent & Child, 10,* 33–34.

Phillips, V. (2011). *Empowering discipline: An approach that works with at-risk students* (3rd ed.). United States: Personal Development Publishing.

Piderit, S., Fry, R., & Cooperrider, D. (Eds.). (2007). *The handbook of transformative cooperation: New designs and dynamics.* Palo Alto, CA: Stanford University Press.

Plata, M., & Masten, W. G. (1998). Teacher ratings of Hispanic and Anglo students on a behavior rating scale. *Roeper Paper, 21,* 139–144.

Pohan, C. A., & Aguilar, T. E. (2001). Measuring educators' beliefs about diversity in personal and professional contexts. *American Educational Research Journal, 38,* 159–182.

Posner, G. J. (2005). *Field experience: A guide to reflective teaching* (6th ed.). Boston: Allyn and Bacon.

Prawat, R. S. (1990). *Changing schools by changing teachers' beliefs about teaching and learning.* East Lansing, MI: Center for the Learning and Teaching of Elementary Subjects Institute for Research on Teaching.

Purkey, W. W. (1979). *Self concept and school achievement.* Englewood Cliffs, NJ: Prentice Hall.

Raths, J. (2001). Teachers' beliefs and teaching beliefs. *Early Childhood Research and Practice, 3.* Available at ecrp.uiuc.edu/v3n1/raths.html

Raths, J., & McAninch, A. C. (Eds.). (2003). *Teacher beliefs and classroom performance: The impact of teacher education: Vol. 6. Advances in Teacher Education.* Greenwich, CT: Information Age Publishing.

Rhem, J. (1999, February). Pygmalion in the classroom. *The National Teaching and Learning Forum*, 8. Available at cte.udel.edu/sites/udel.edu.cte/files/ntlf/v8n2/pygmalion.htm

Richards, J. C., Gallo, P. B., & Renandya, W. A. (2001). Exploring teachers' beliefs and the processes of change. *PAC Journal, 1*, 41–62.

Richardson, V., Anders, P., Tidwell, D., & Lloyd, C. (1991). The relationship between teachers' beliefs and practices in reading comprehension instruction. *American Educational Research Journal, 28, 559–586.*

Rosenthal, R., & Jacobson, L. (1968). *Pygmalion in the classroom: Teachers' expectations and pupils' intellectual development*. New York: Holt, Rinehart and Winston.

Rutter, M. (1979). Protective factors in children's responses to stress and disadvantaged. In M. W. Kent & J. E. Rolf (Eds.), *Primary prevention of psychopathology: Social competence in children* (pp. 49–74). Oxford, UK: Blackwell.

Rutter, M. (1987). Psychosocial resilience and protective mechanisms. *American Journal of Orthopsychiatry, 57, 316–331.*

Rutter, M. (2006). Implications of resilience concepts for scientific understanding. In B. M. Lester, A. S. Masten, & B. McEwen (Vol. Eds.), *Annals of the New York Academy of Sciences: Vol. 1094. Resilience in children* (pp. 1–12). Malden, MA: Blackwell Publishing.

Rutter, M. (2012). Resilience as a dynamic concept. *Development and Psychopathology, 24, 335–344.*

Rutter, M., Maughan, B., Mortimore, P., Ouston, J., & Smith, A. (1979). *Fifteen thousand hours: Secondary schools and their effects on children*. Cambridge, MA: Harvard University Press.

Ryan, A., & Patrick, H. (2001). The classroom social environment and changes in adolescents' motivation and engagement during middle school. *American Educational Research Journal, 38, 437–460.*

Sameroff, A. J., Gutman, L., & Peck, S. C. (2003). Adaptation among young facing multiple risks: Prospective research findings. In S. S. Luthar (Ed.), *Resilience and vulnerability: Adaptation in the context of childhood adversities* (pp. 364–391). New York: Cambridge University Press.

Schaps, E. (2000). Building community from within. *Principal, 80,* 14–17.

Schaps, E. (2003). The heart of a caring school. *Educational Leadership, 60,* 31–33.

Schirmer, B. R., Casbon, J., & Twiss, L. L. (1997). Teacher beliefs about learning: What happens when the child doesn't fit the schema? *The Reading Teacher, 50,* 690–692.

Schon, D. A., (Ed.). (1991). *The reflective turn: Case studies in and on educational practice*. New York: Teachers College Press.

Schultz, J., & Cook-Sather, A. (Eds.). (2001). *In our own words: Students' perspectives on school*. Lanham, MD: Rowman and Littlefield Publishers, Inc.

Schunk, D. H. (1982). Effects of effort attributional feedback on children's perceived self-efficacy and achievement. *Journal of Educational Psychology, 74,* 548–556.

Selig, W. G., Arroyo, A. A., Lloyd-Zannini, L. P., & Jordan, H. (2006*). Handbook of individualized strategies for building resiliency in at-risk students.* Los Angeles: Western Psychological Services.

Seligman, M., & Csikszentmihalyi, M. (2000). Positive psychology: An introduction. *American Psychologist, 55,* 5–14.

Senge, P. (1990). *The art and practice of the learning organization.* New York: Doubleday.

Shonkoff, J. P., Garner, A. S., & Committee on Psychosocial Aspects of Child and Family Health, Committee on Early Childhood, Adoption, and Dependent Care, and Section on Developmental and Behavioral Pediatrics. (2012). The lifelong effects of early childhood adversity and toxic stress. *Pediatrics, 129,* e232–e246.

Siegel, D. (2010). *Mindsight: The new science of personal transformation.* New York: Random House.

Strucker, M., & Moise, L. N., Magee, V., & Kreider, H. (2001). Writing the wrong: Making schools better for girls. In J. Schultz & A. Cook-Sather (Eds.), *In our own words: Students' perspectives on school* (pp. 149–164). Lanham, MD: Rowman & Littlefield Publishers, Inc.

Tatto, M. T. (1996). Examining values and beliefs about teaching diverse students: Understanding the challenges for teacher education. *Educational Evaluation and Policy Analysis, 18,* 155–180.

Thapa, T., Cohen, J., Guffey, S., & Higgins-D'Alessandro, A. (2013). A review of school climate research. *Review of Educational Research.* Available at rer.sagepub.com/content/early/2013/04/18/0034654313483907

Truebridge, S. (2010). *Tell me a story: Influencing educators' beliefs about student resilience in an effort to enhance student success.* (Doctoral dissertation). Available from Dissertations and Theses database. (UMI No. 3408480)

Tschannen-Moran, M., & Hoy, W. K. (1998). Trust in schools: A conceptual and empirical analysis. *Journal of Educational Administration, 36,* 334–352.

Ungar, M. (2004). A constructionist discourse on resilience: Multiple contexts, multiple realities among at-risk children and youth. *Youth & Society, 35,* 341–365.

Vodicka, D. (2006). The four elements of trust: Consistency, compassion, communication, and competency. *Principal Leadership,* 27–30.

Vygotsky, L. (1978). *Mind in society.* Cambridge, MA: Harvard University Press.

Walsh, J. (1997). *The eye of the storm: Ten years on the front lines of new futures. An interview with Otis Johnson and Don Crary.* Baltimore, MD: Annie E. Casey Foundation.

Watkins, J. M., & Mohr, B. J. (2001). *Appreciative inquiry: Change at the speed of imagination.* San Francisco: Jossey-Bass/Pfeiffer.

Waxman, H. C., Padron, Y. N., & Gray, J. P. (Eds.). (2004). *Educational resiliency: Student, teacher, and school perspectives.* Greenwich, CT: Information Age Publishing.

Wehmiller, P. L. (1992, Fall). Teaching and practice: When the walls come tumbling down. *Harvard Education Review, 62,* 373–383.

Weiner, B. (1990). History of motivational research in education. *Journal of Educational Psychology, 82,* 616–622.

Wenger, E., McDermott, R., & Snyder, W. (2002). *Cultivating communities of practice.* Boston: Harvard Business School Press.

Werner, E. (2005). Resilience and recovery: Findings from the Kauai Longitudinal Study. *Focal Point: Research, Policy, and Practice in Children's Mental Health, 19.* Available at pathwaysrtc.pdx.edu/focalpointS05.shtml

Werner, E., & Smith, R. (1989). *Vulnerable but invincible: A longitudinal study of resilient children and youth.* New York: Adams, Bannister, and Cox.

Werner, E., & Smith, R., (1992). *Overcoming the odds: High-risk children from birth to adulthood.* Ithaca, NY: Cornell University Press.

Westheimer, K., Abeles, V., & Truebridge, S. (2011). *End the race: Facilitation guide and companion resource to the film* Race to Nowhere. Lafayette, CA: Reel Link Films.

Wolin, S., & Wolin, S. J. (1999). *Shaping a brighter future by uncovering "survivor's pride."* Available at projectresilience.com/article19.htm

Yero, J. L. (2002). *Teaching in mind: How teacher thinking shapes education.* Hamilton, MT: Mindflight Publishing.

Index

About the Author

Sara Truebridge is a consultant and researcher specializing in the area of resilience, combining her experience and expertise in research, policy, and practice to promote success and equity for all. She has consulted and worked with the U.S. Department of Education and has given numerous presentations, webinars, and workshops throughout the United States. She (with Bonnie Benard) is coauthor of a number of articles and publications on resilience. Truebridge was the 2011 recipient of the American Educational Research Association (AERA) Excellence in Research to Practice Award, awarded by the Special Interest Group (SIG): Research Use. She is also one of two international recipients of the 2005 Howard M. Soule Fellowship for Doctoral Studies: a Phi Delta Kappa Graduate Fellowship in Educational Leadership. Truebridge earned a doctorate from Mills College; a teaching credential from California State University, East Bay; and a bachelor's degree in psychology from Denison University. She also graduated from the University of California–Berkeley program Children and the Changing Family and the Harvard Graduate School of Education program Closing the Achievement Gap: Linking Families, Schools, and Communities through Complementary Learning.

Truebridge is the education consultant to the education documentary *Race to Nowhere* and *Love Hate Love,* a documentary about resilience, which was executive produced by Sean Penn and debuted on Oprah Winfrey's network, OWN. Truebridge has over 20 years of classroom experience. She was recognized by the National Education Association (NEA) as one of three outstanding elementary student teachers in the nation. Prior to becoming a teacher, Truebridge was the legislative analyst for education in the New York State Senate and was later appointed by then New York State Governor, Mario Cuomo, to be the special assistant to the New York State secretary of state.

Truebridge resides in California with her husband, Chris, and son, Ian.

She can be reached for professional development, consultations and communication at resilienceST@gmail.com. You can also visit the website Educating the New Humanity at www.EducatingTheNewHumanity.org.